# QUICK KEYBOARD PICTURE CHORDS

## By HOLLEY GENE LEFFLER

The method of diagramming chords in music has evolved haphazardly. That is why there are several symbols for some of the chords.

There is a movement to standardize the symbols, but there is no standard consensus on whether the chord symbol should reflect the melody plus the harmony (both hands) or just the harmony (left hand).

To make chords easier to read in this book, I have

- moved chord inversions around to keep the notes within the staff
- expressed chords enharmonically (see Info Page) at times to avoid double flats and double sharps

In this book, I give you many options to make chords quickly and easily. It's an easy book to use that will grow with any piano/keyboard/organ player.

*Holley Gene Leffler*

## Conte

*Interior photos by James Bean, Ojai, CA.*

Catalog No. 07-2040
ISBN# 1-56922-118-9

EXCLUSIVELY DISTRIBUTED BY

7777 W. BLUEMOUND RD. P.O. BOX 13819 MILWAUKEE, WI 53213

Visit Hal Leonard Online at
**www.halleonard.com**

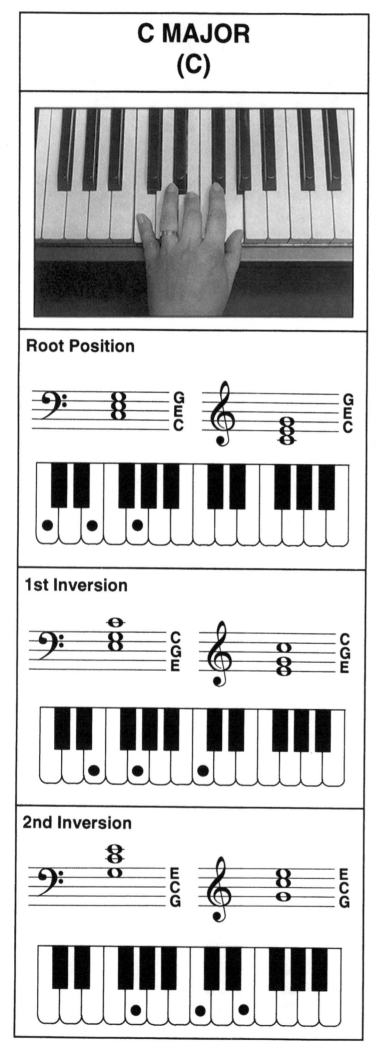

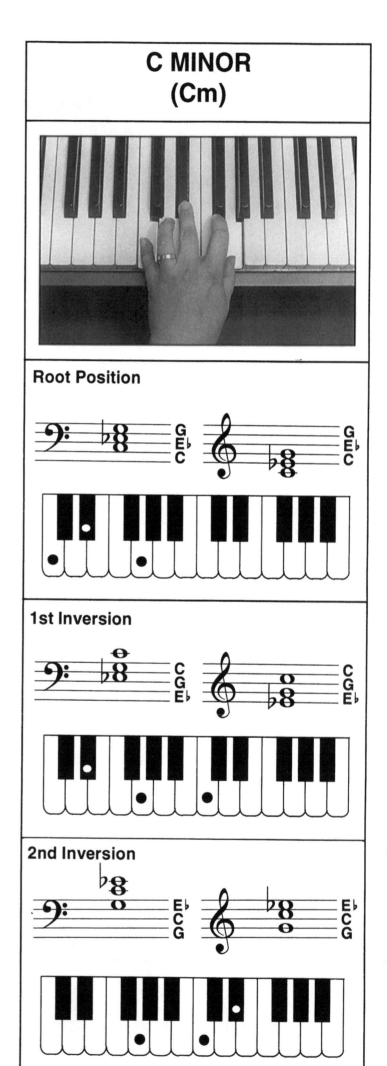

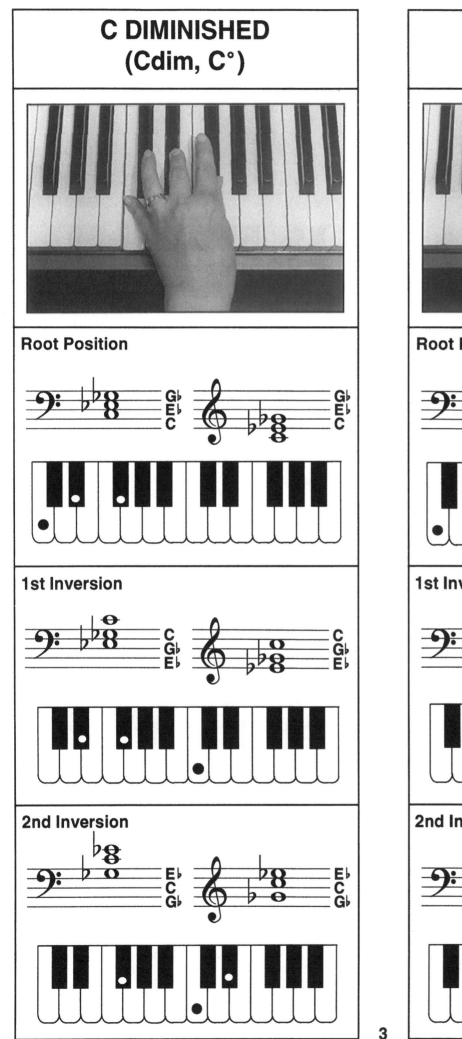

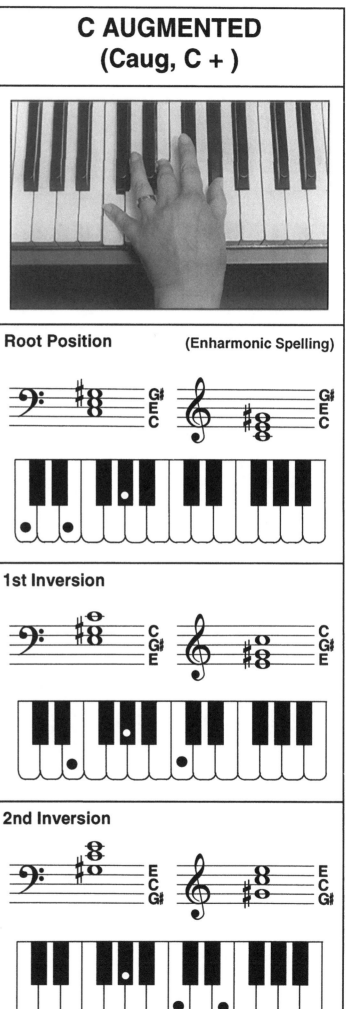

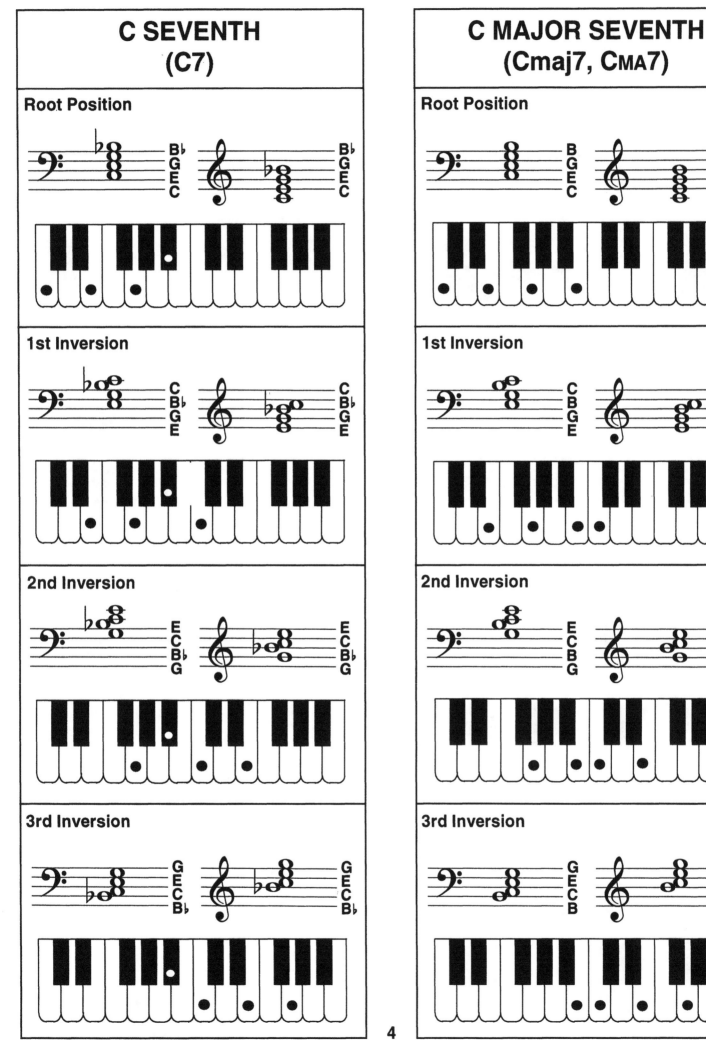

# C SEVENTH
## (C7)

**Root Position**

BGEC
BGEC

**1st Inversion**

CBB♭GE
CBB♭GE

**2nd Inversion**

ECB♭G
ECB♭G

**3rd Inversion**

GECB♭
GECB♭

# C MAJOR SEVENTH
## (Cmaj7, Cма7)

**Root Position**

BGEC
BGEC

**1st Inversion**

CBGE
CBGE

**2nd Inversion**

ECBG
ECBG

**3rd Inversion**

GECB
GECB

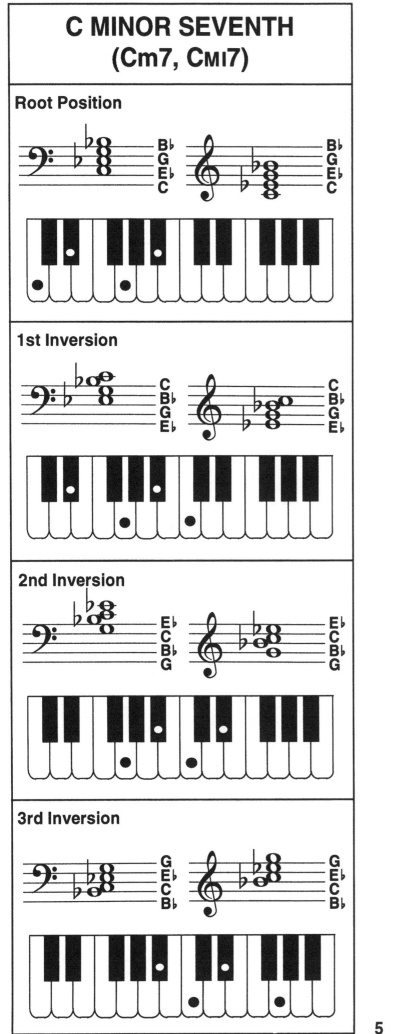

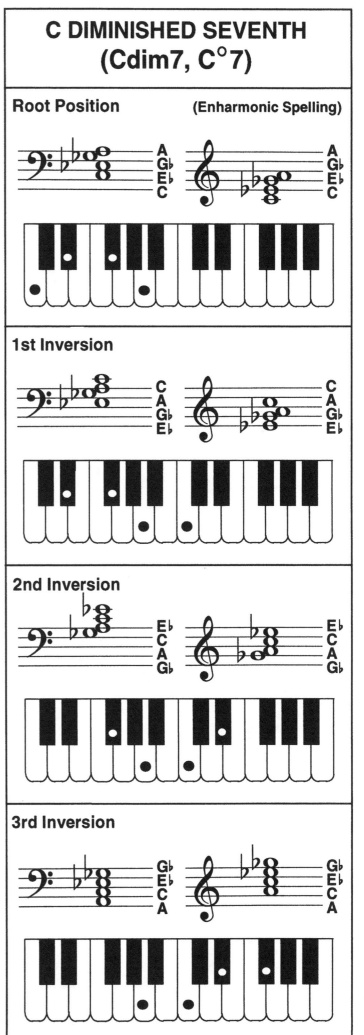

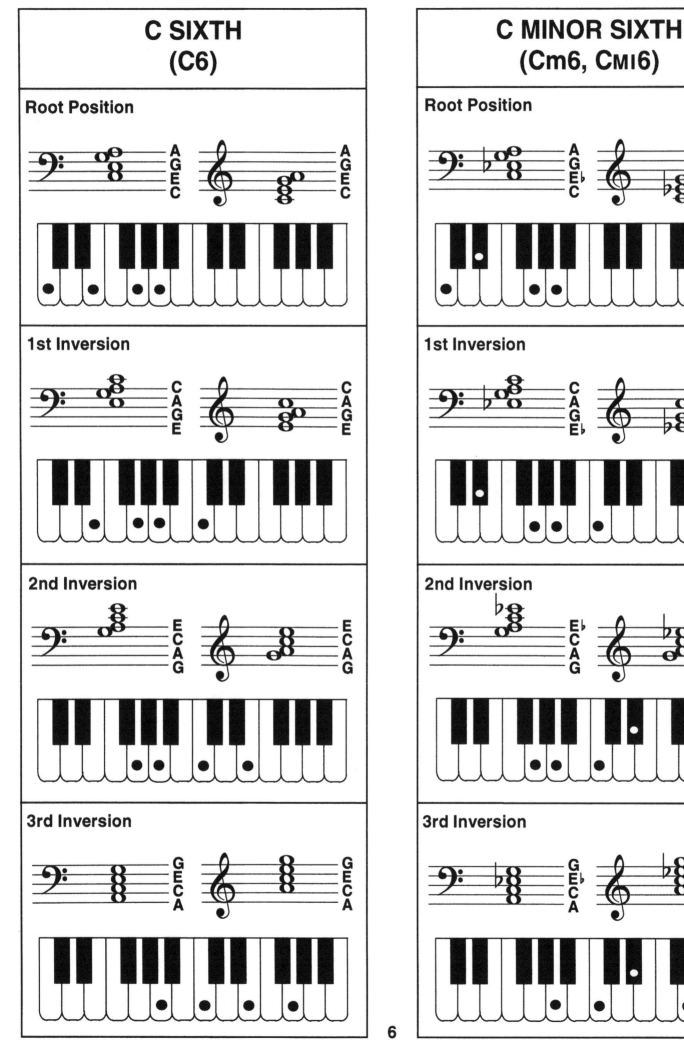

6

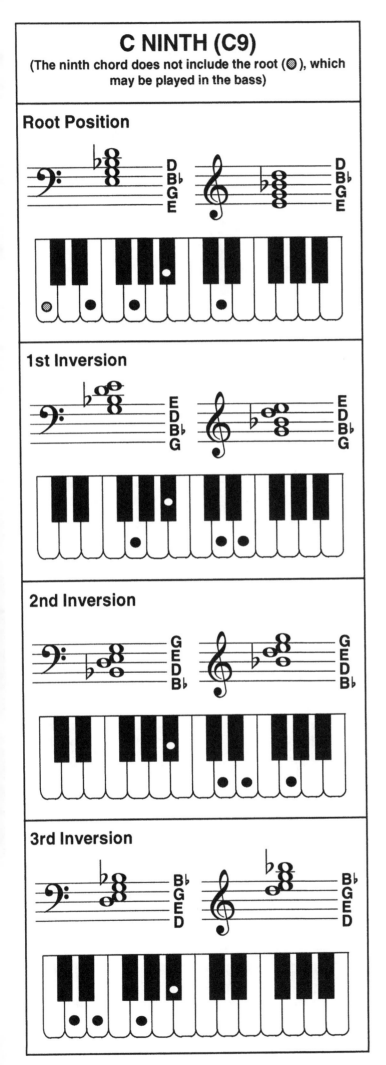

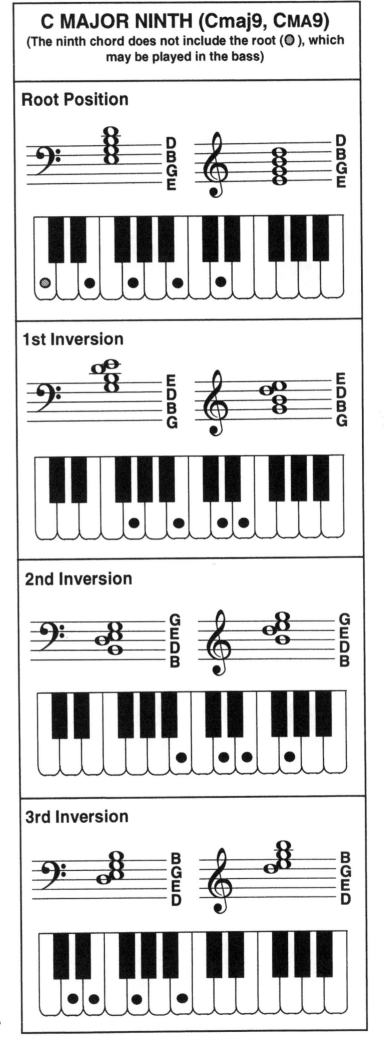

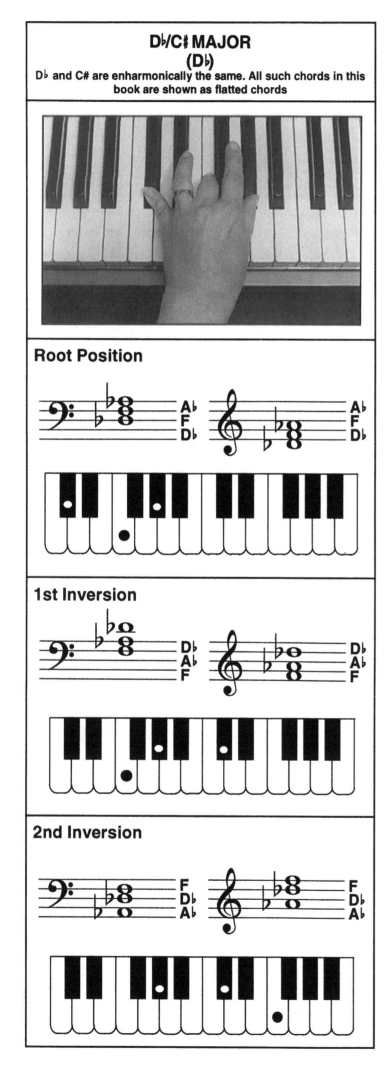

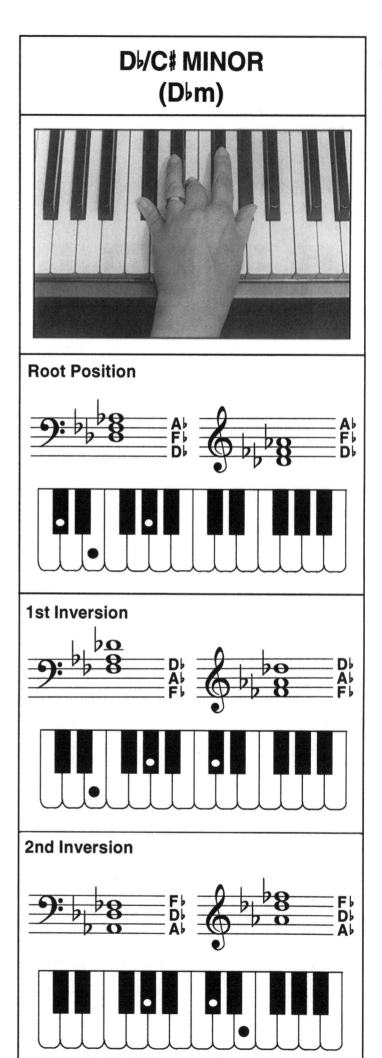

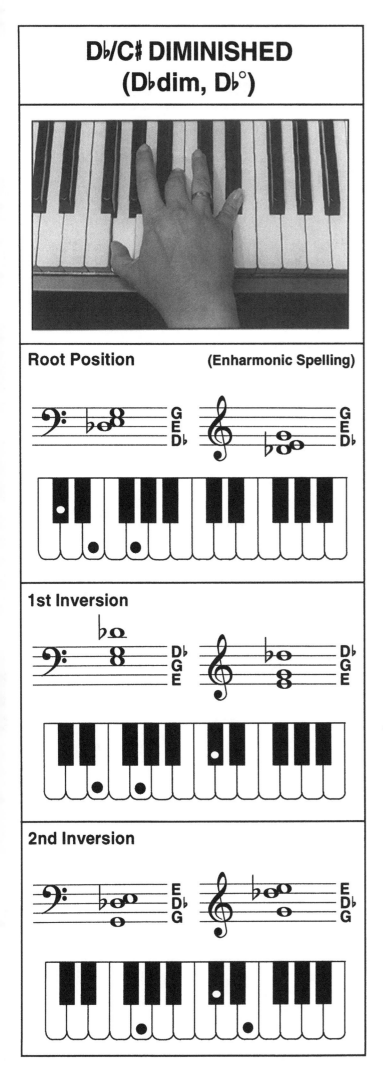

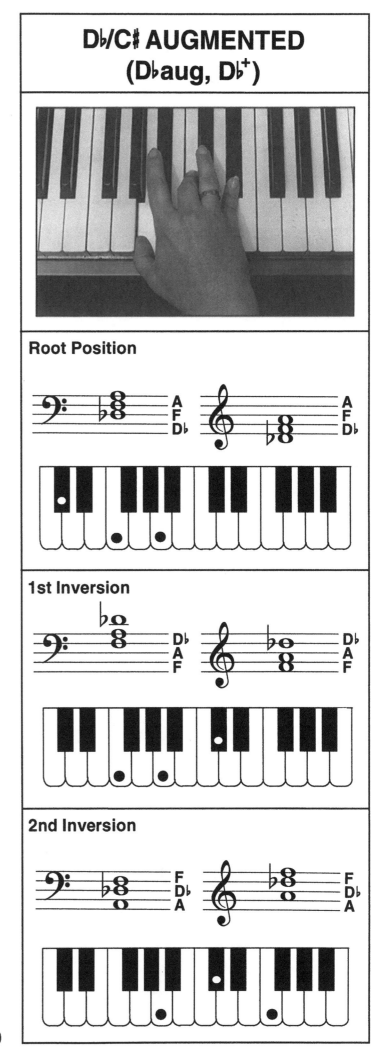

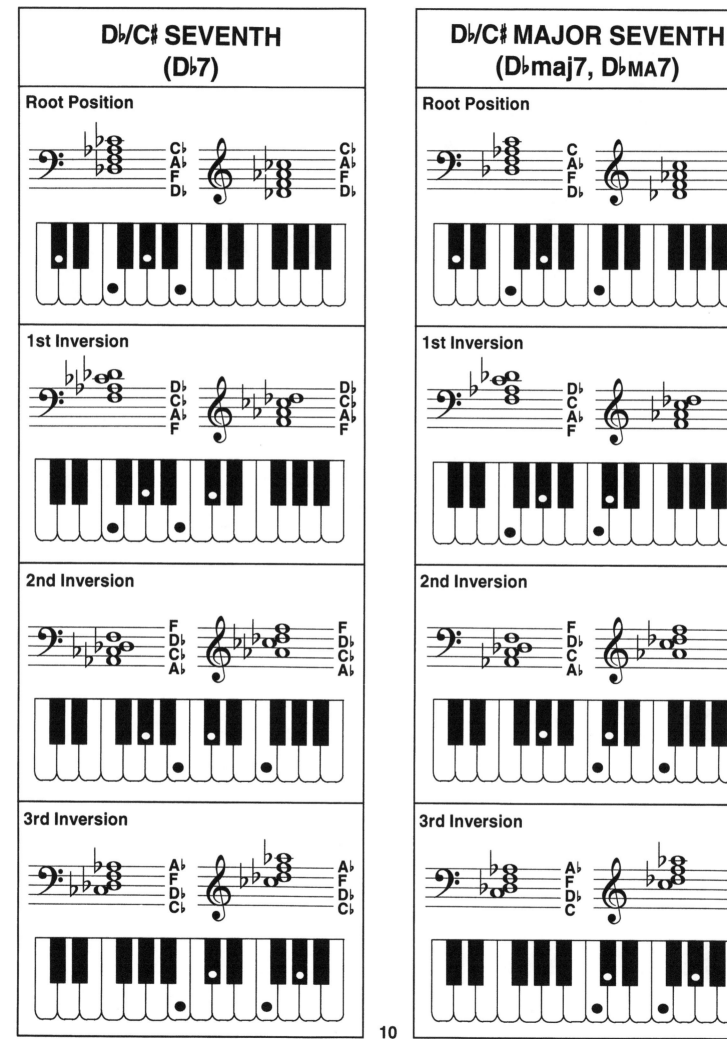

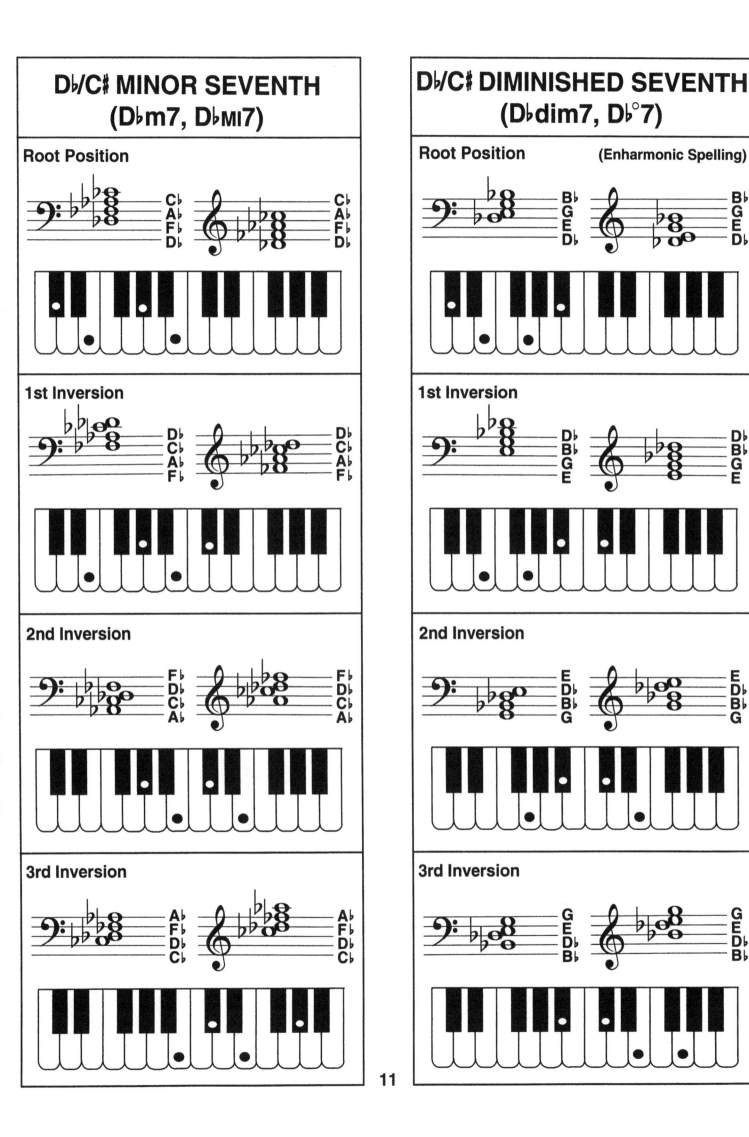

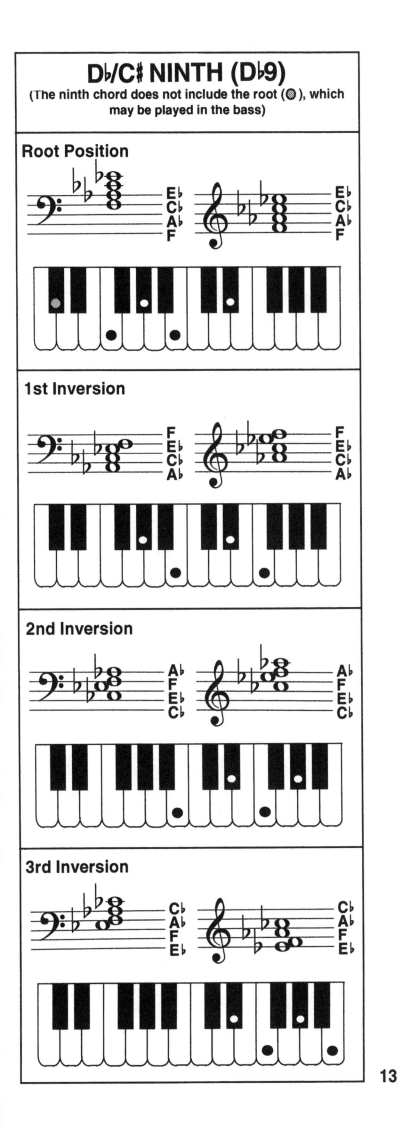

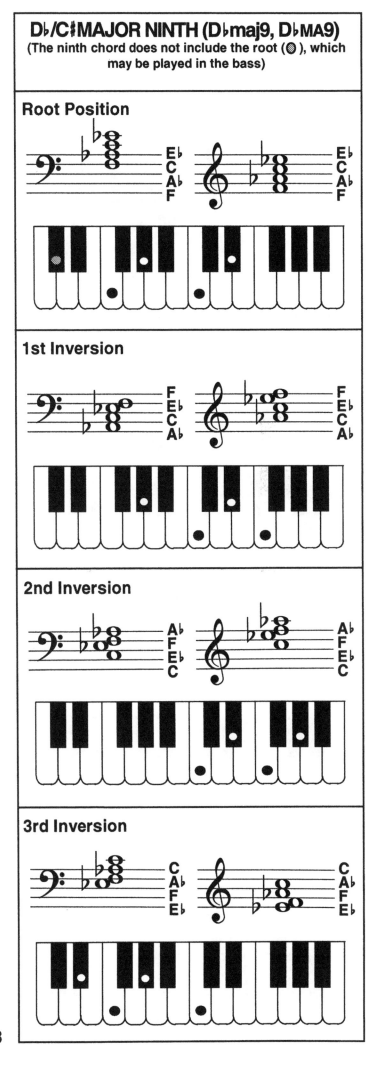

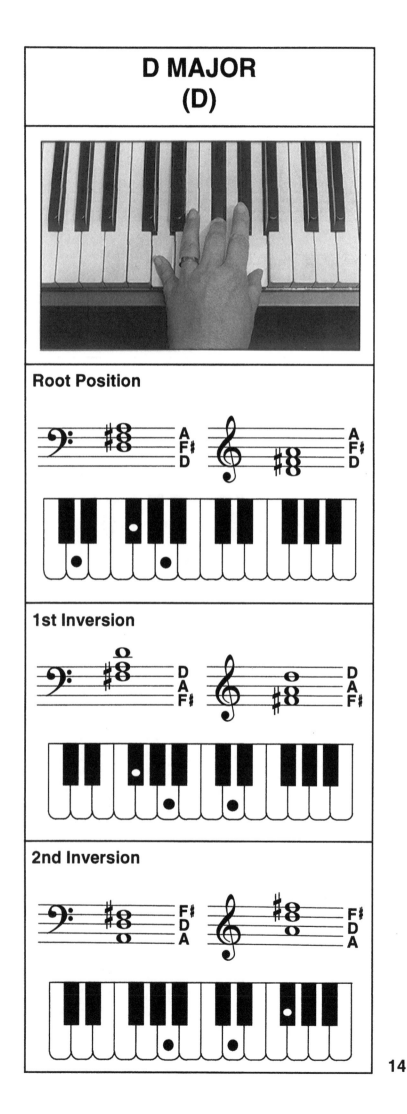
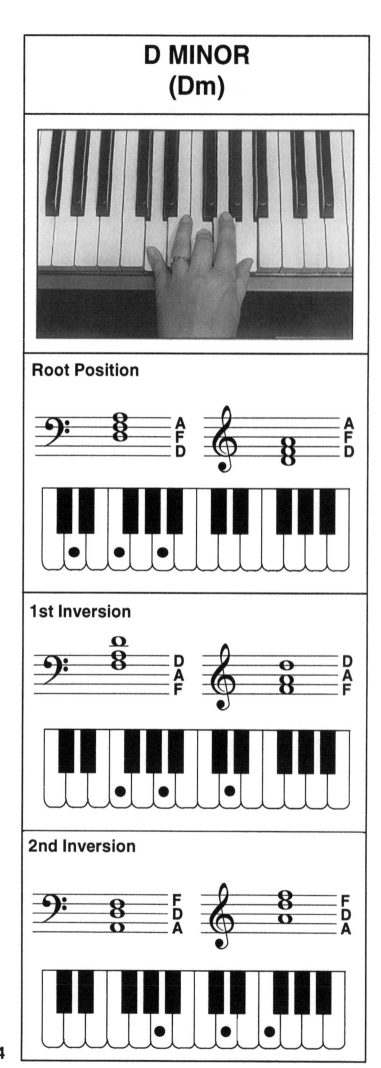

14

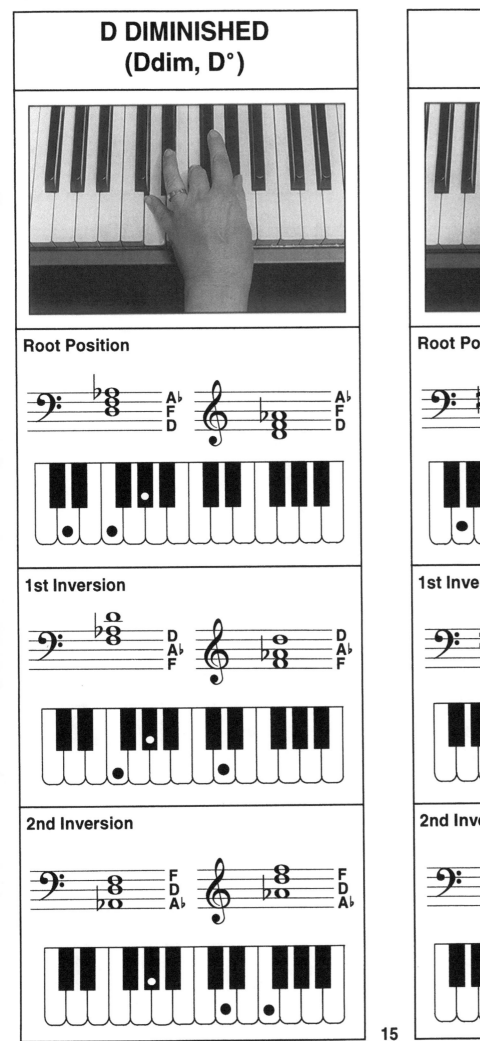
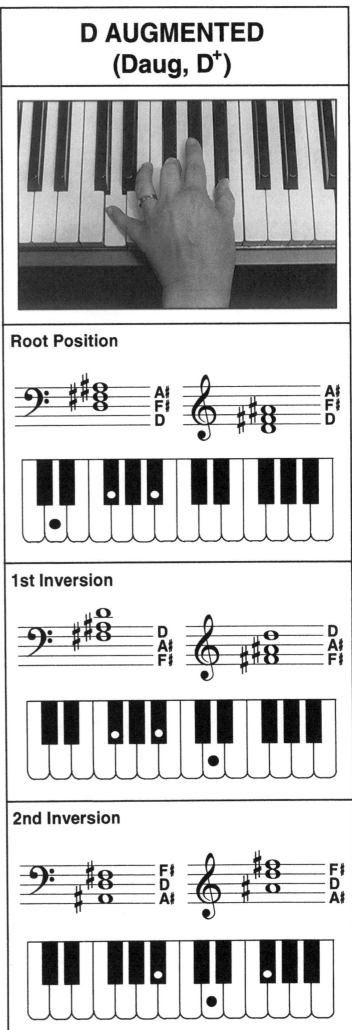

# D MINOR SEVENTH
## (Dm7, DmI7)

### Root Position

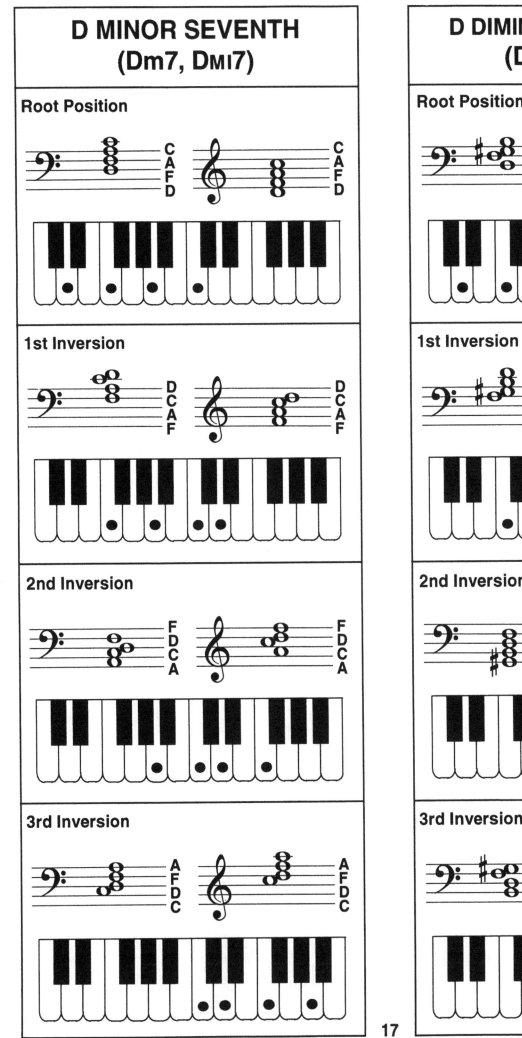

### 1st Inversion

### 2nd Inversion

### 3rd Inversion

# D DIMINISHED SEVENTH
## (Ddim7, D°7)

### Root Position      (Enharmonic Spelling)

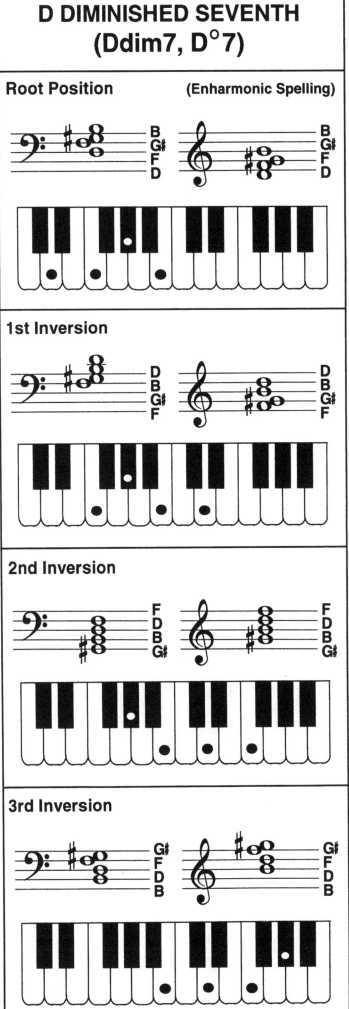

### 1st Inversion

### 2nd Inversion

### 3rd Inversion

17

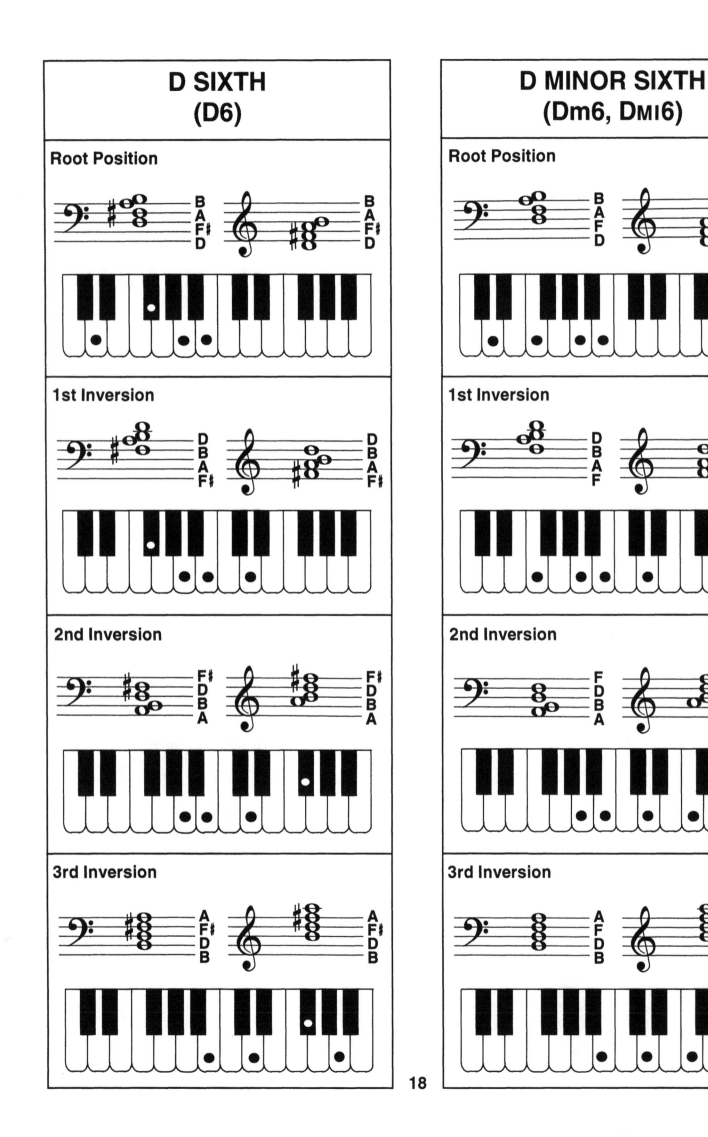

# D SIXTH
## (D6)

**Root Position**

**1st Inversion**

**2nd Inversion**

**3rd Inversion**

# D MINOR SIXTH
## (Dm6, Dmi6)

**Root Position**

**1st Inversion**

**2nd Inversion**

**3rd Inversion**

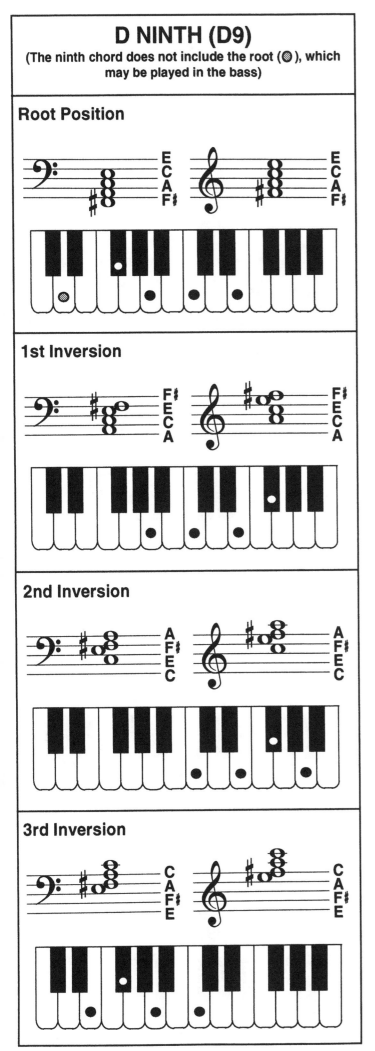

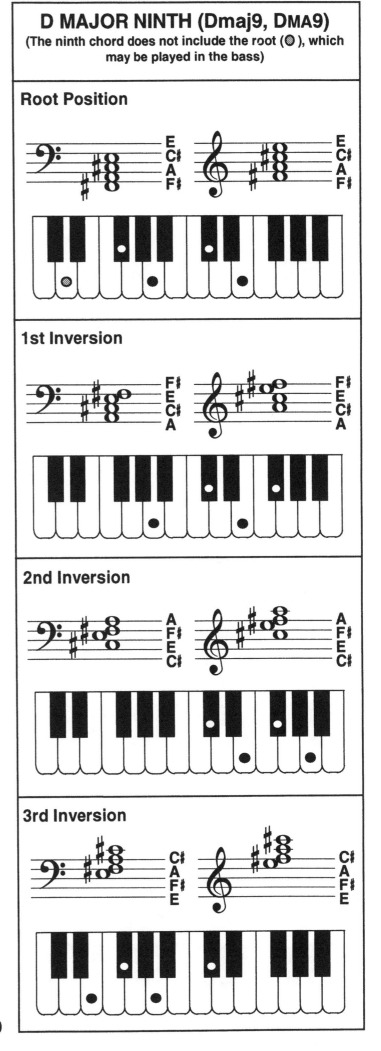

19

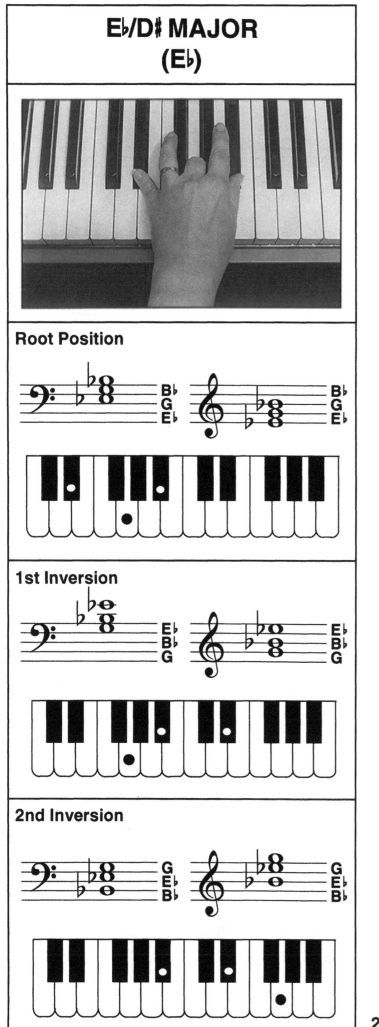

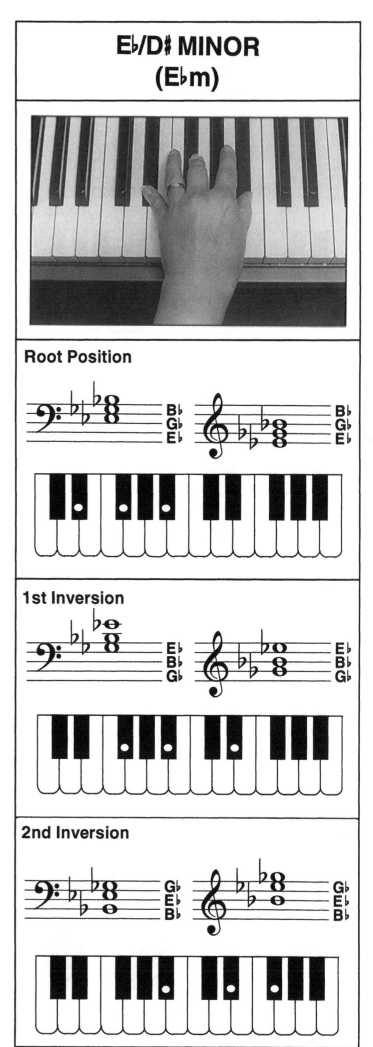

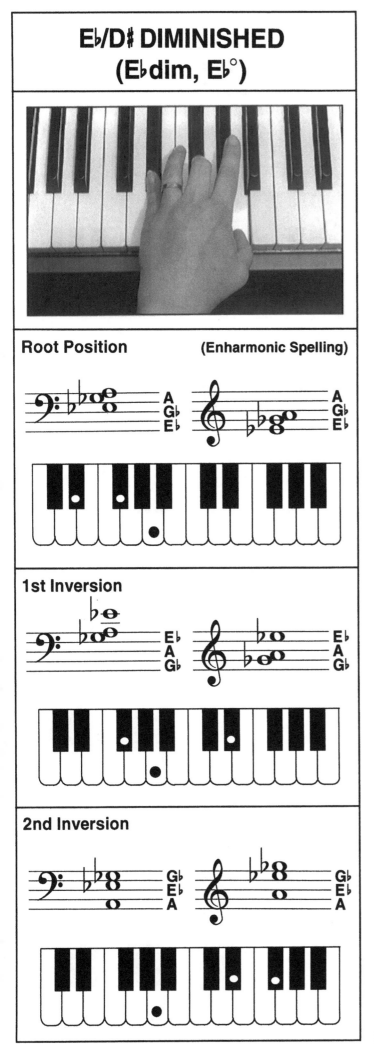

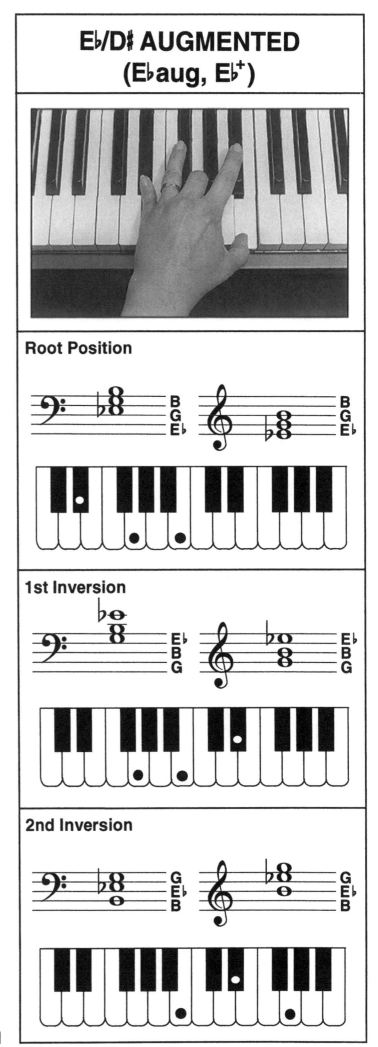

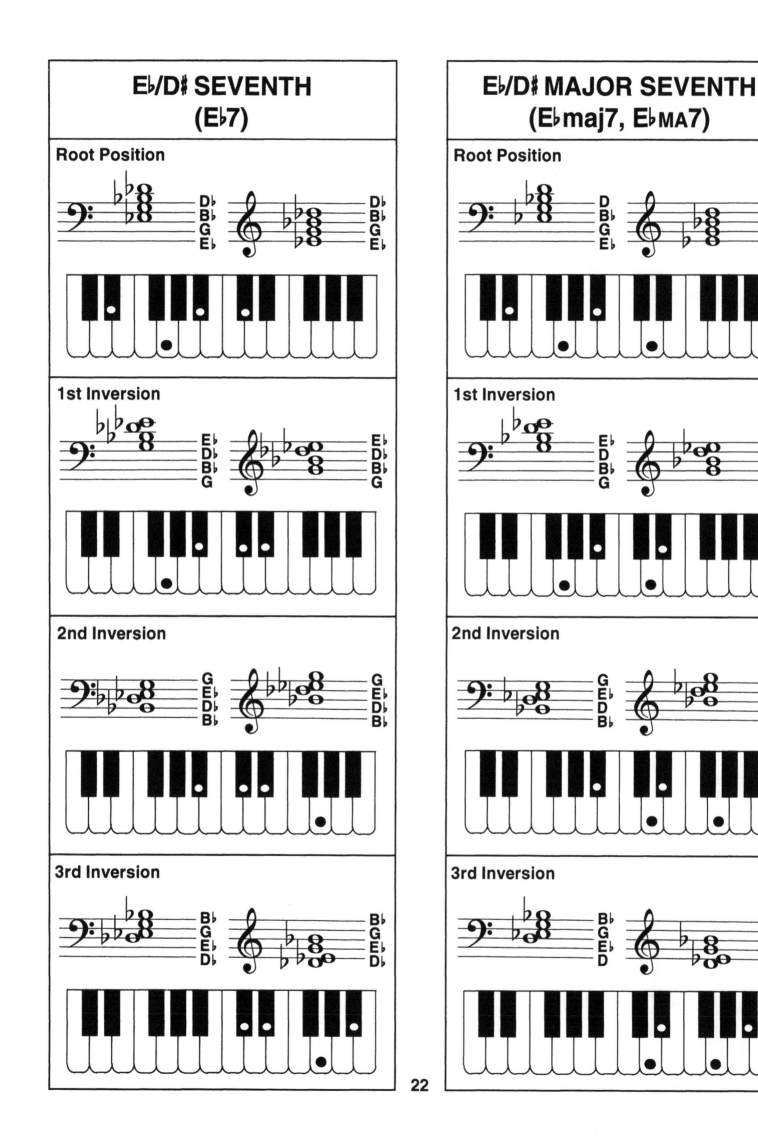

22

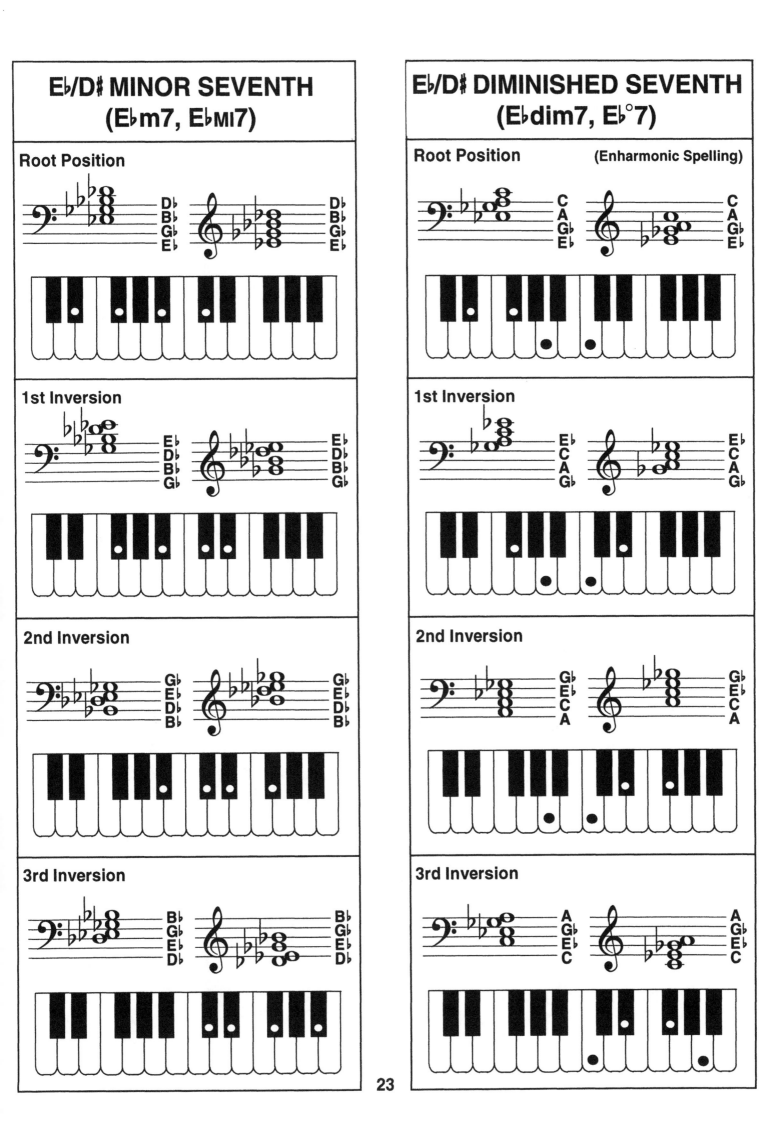

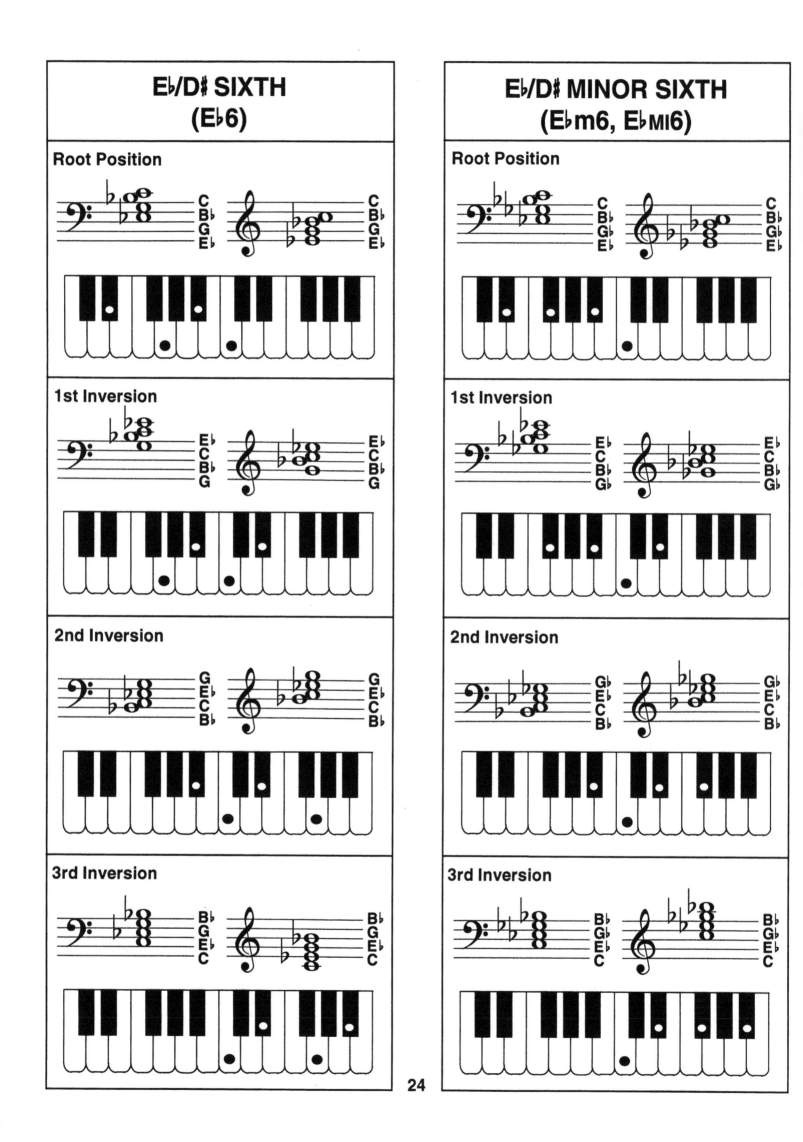

# E♭/D♯ NINTH (E♭9)
### (The ninth chord does not include the root (◉), which may be played in the bass)

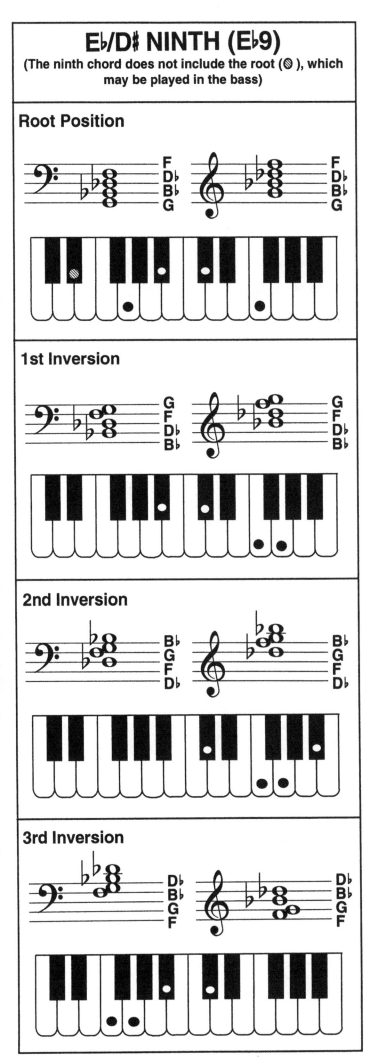

# E♭/D♯ MAJOR NINTH (E♭maj9, E♭MA9)
### (The ninth chord does not include the root (◉), which may be played in the bass)

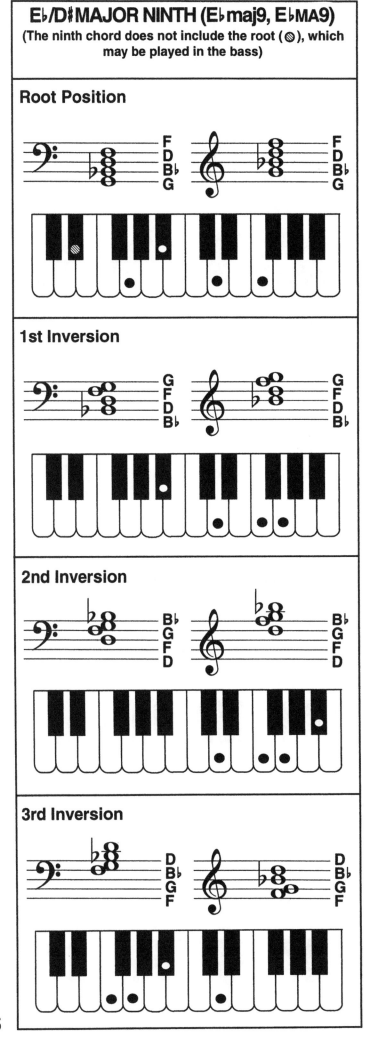

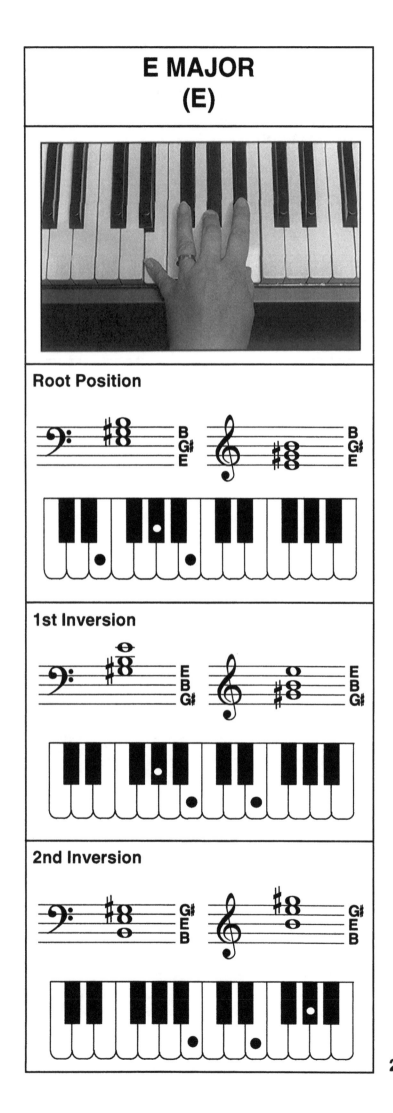

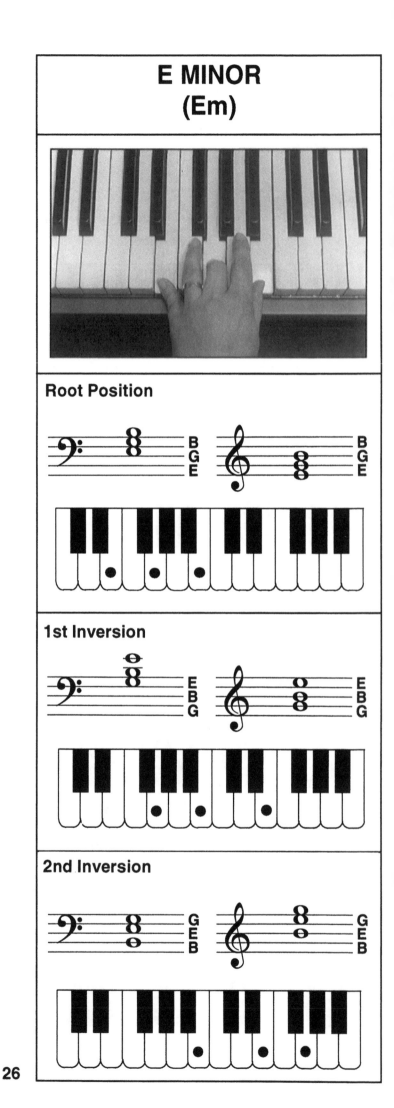

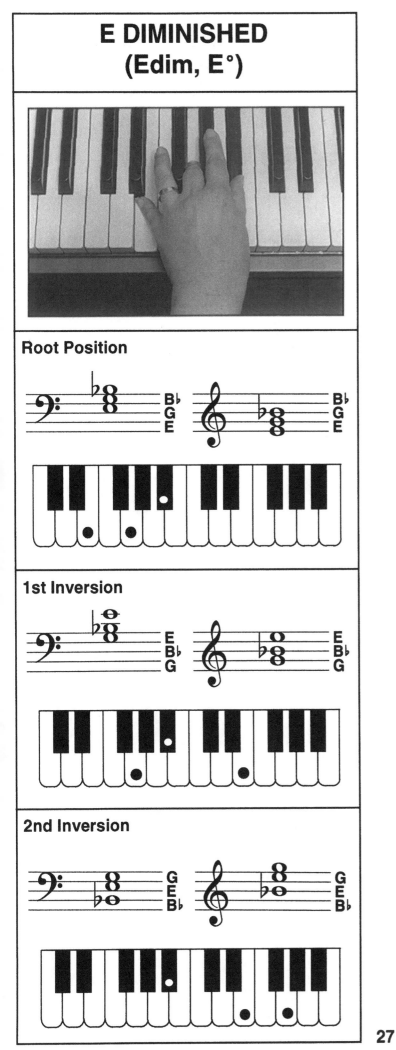

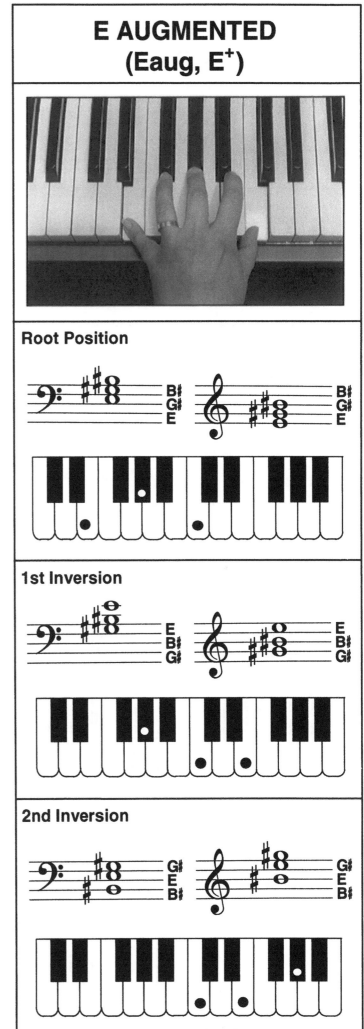

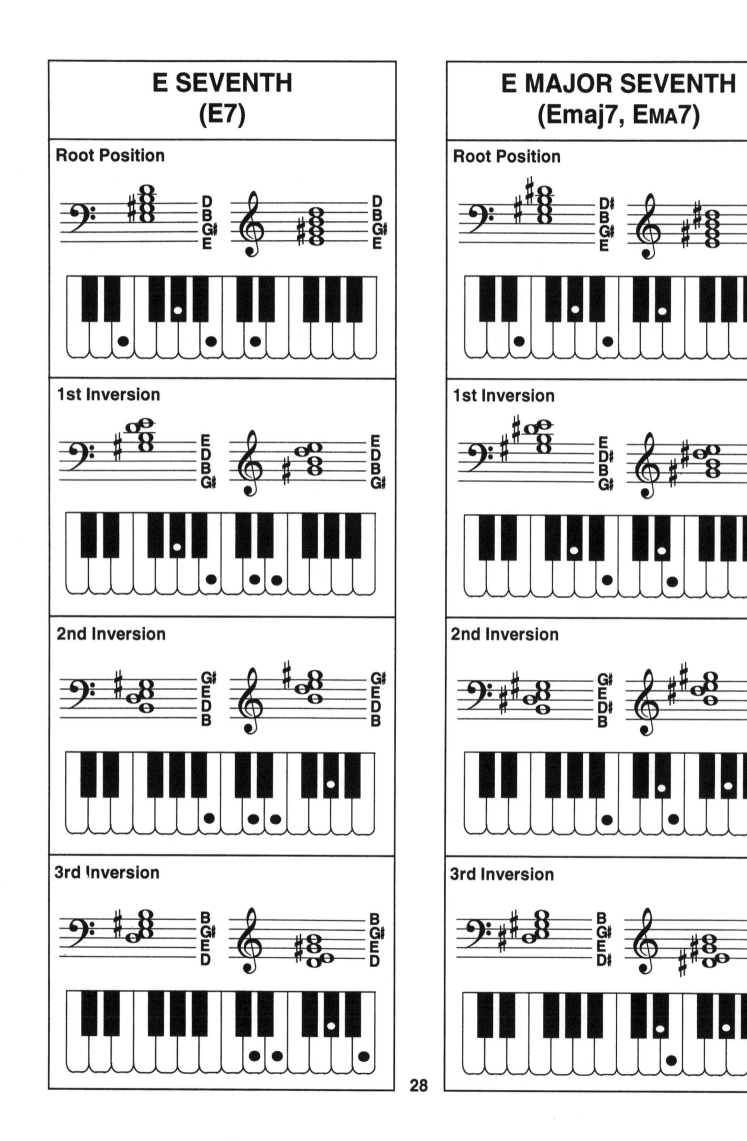

28

# E MINOR SEVENTH
## (Em7, Emi7)

**Root Position**

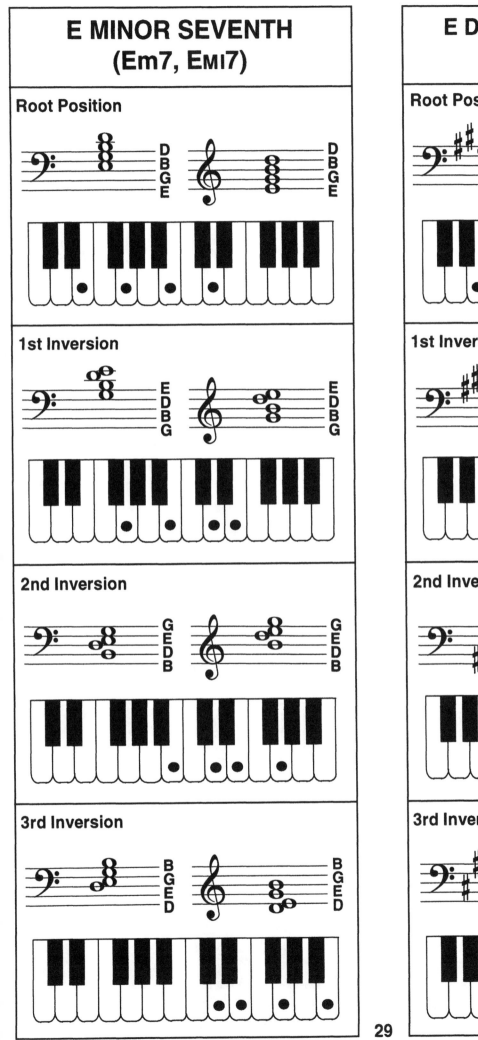

**1st Inversion**

**2nd Inversion**

**3rd Inversion**

# E DIMINISHED SEVENTH
## (Edim7, E°7)

**Root Position**          (Enharmonic Spelling)

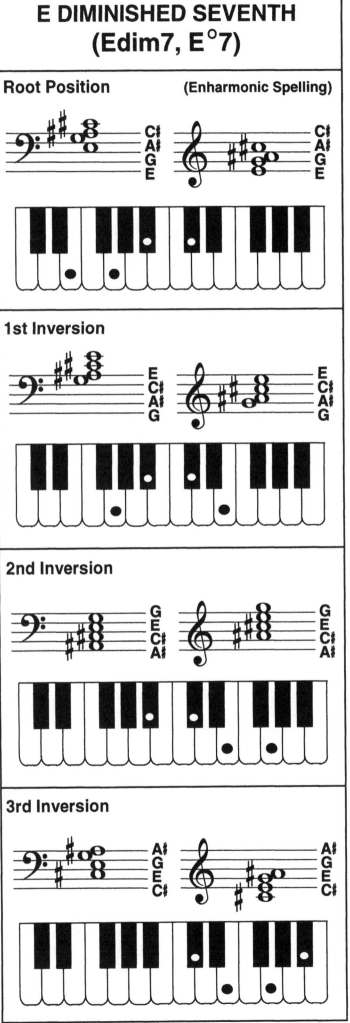

**1st Inversion**

**2nd Inversion**

**3rd Inversion**

# E SIXTH
## (E6)

### Root Position

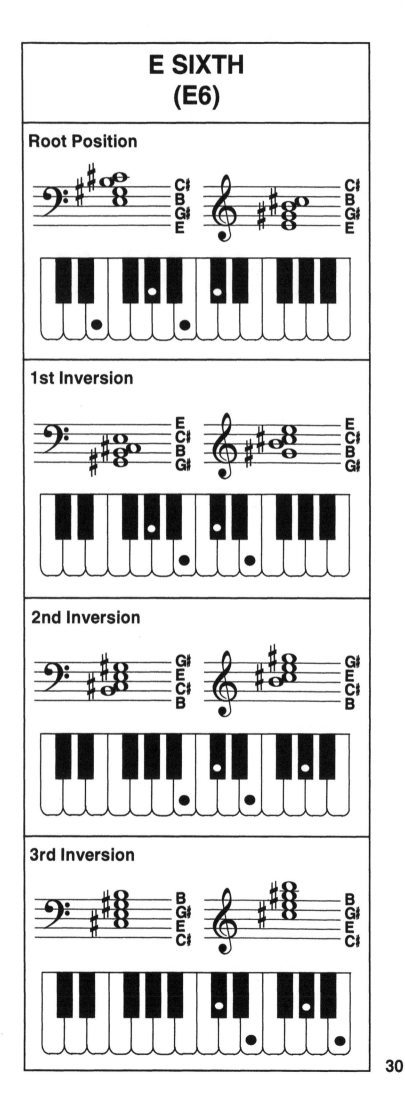

### 1st Inversion

### 2nd Inversion

### 3rd Inversion

# E MINOR SIXTH
## (Em6, Emi6)

### Root Position

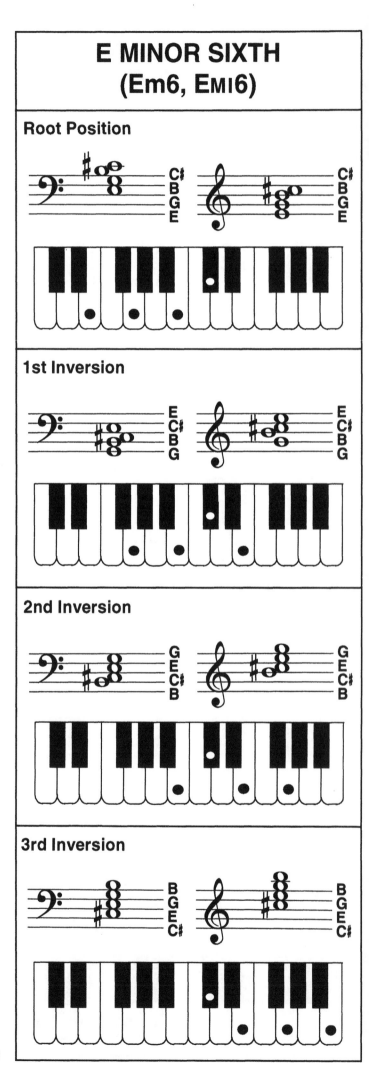

### 1st Inversion

### 2nd Inversion

### 3rd Inversion

30

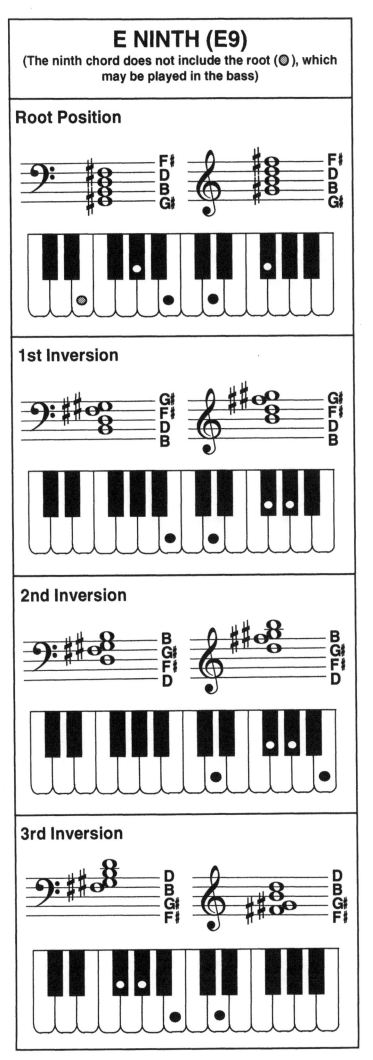

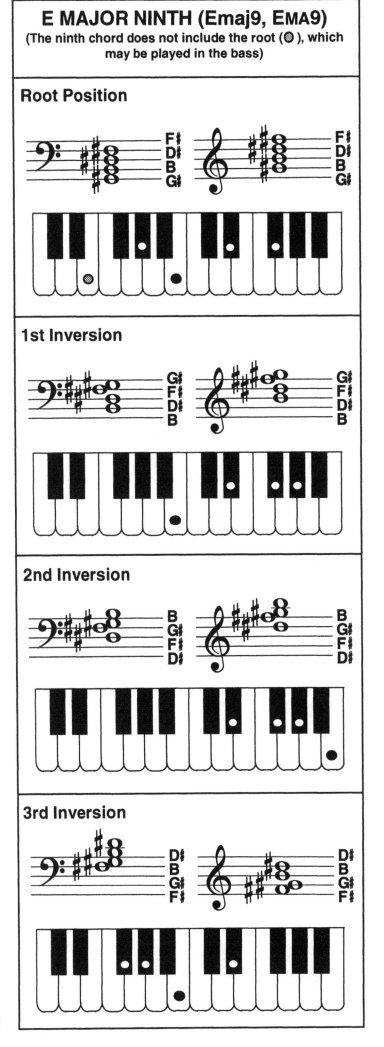

31

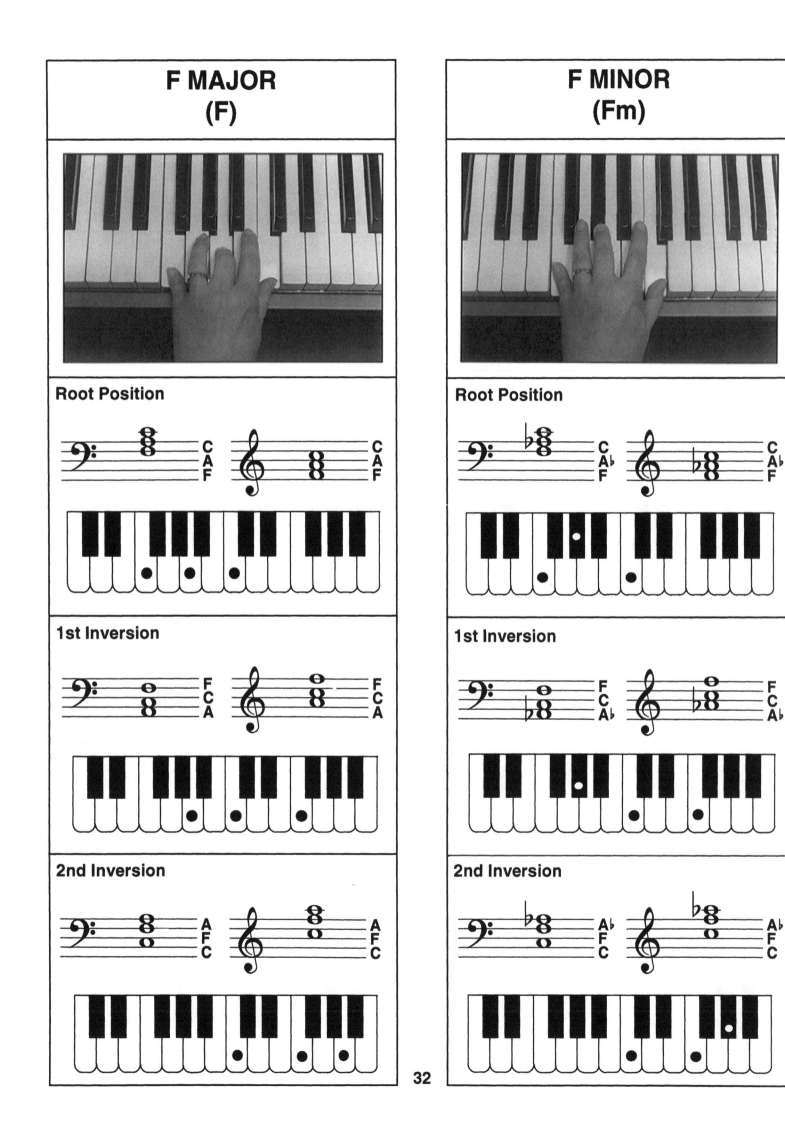

# F DIMINISHED
## (Fdim, F°)

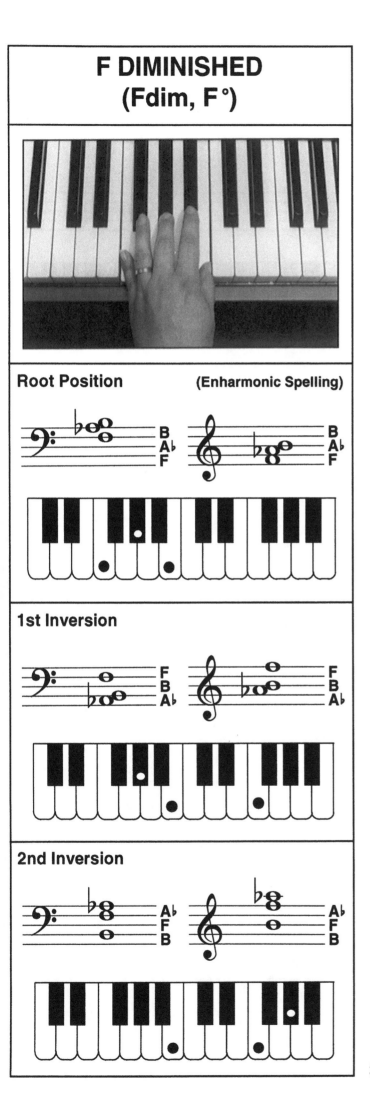

**Root Position**       (Enharmonic Spelling)

B
A♭
F

**1st Inversion**

F
B
A♭

**2nd Inversion**

A♭
F
B

# F AUGMENTED
## (Faug, F⁺)

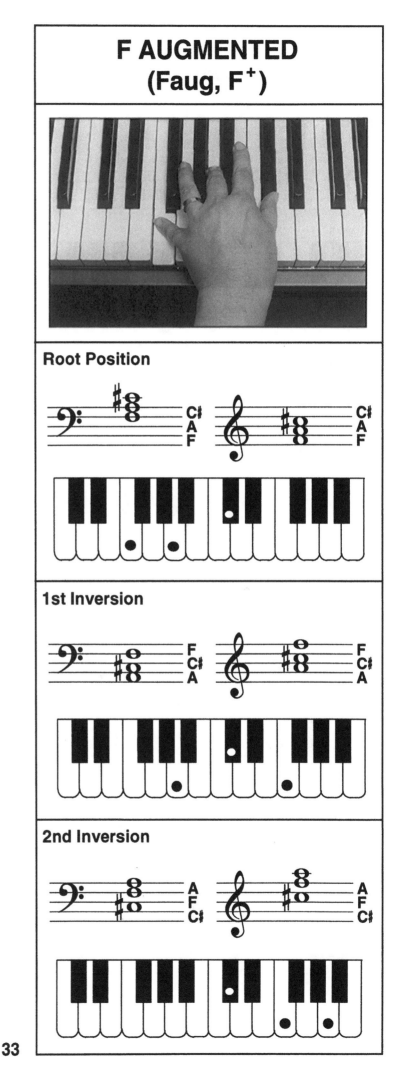

**Root Position**

C♯
A
F

**1st Inversion**

F
C♯
A

**2nd Inversion**

A
F
C♯

33

# F SEVENTH
## (F7)

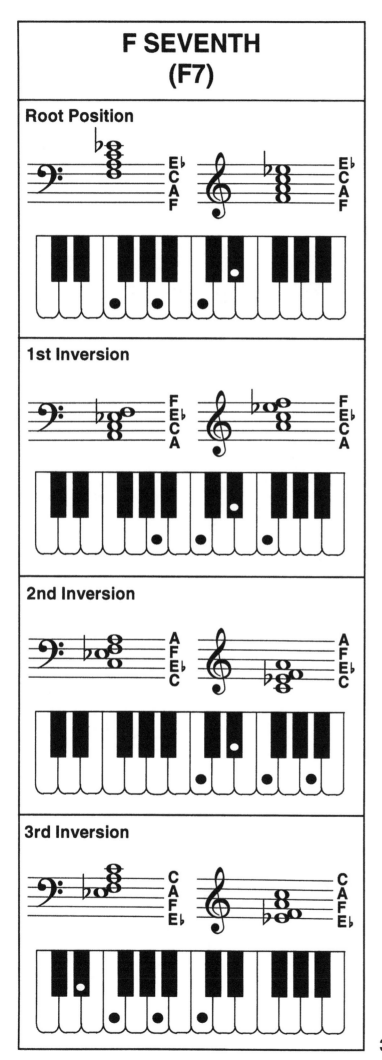

# F MAJOR SEVENTH
## (Fmaj7, FMA7)

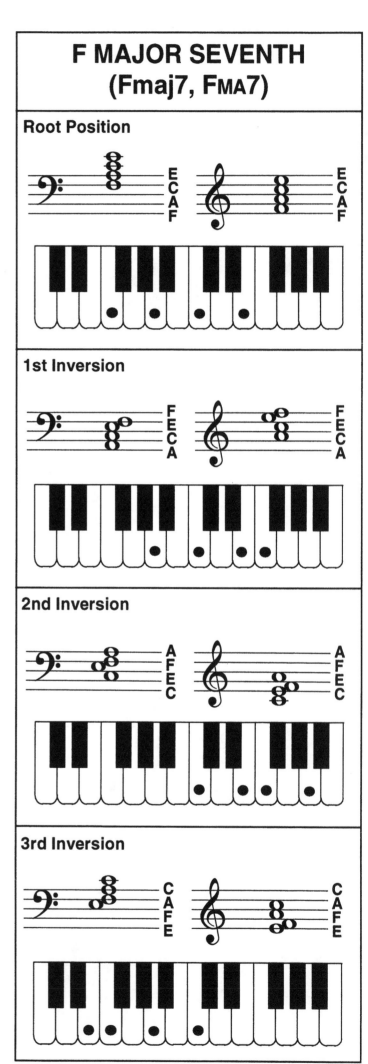

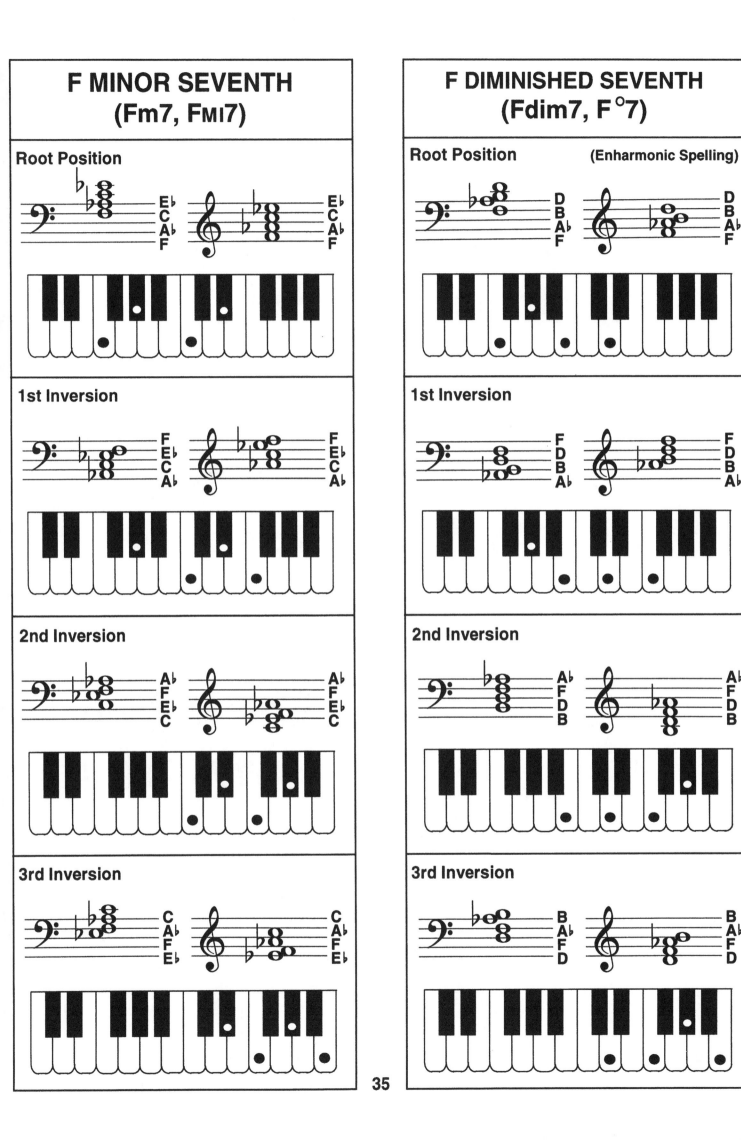

35

## F SIXTH
### (F6)

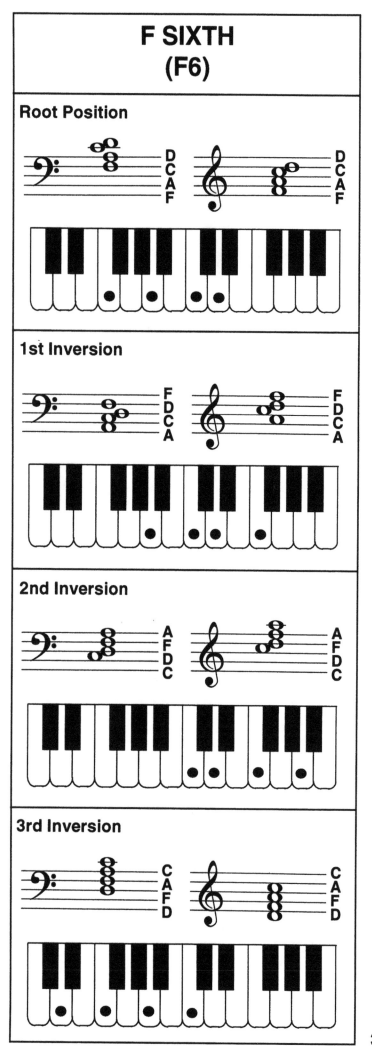

**Root Position**

**1st Inversion**

**2nd Inversion**

**3rd Inversion**

## F MINOR SIXTH
### (Fm6, Fᴍɪ6)

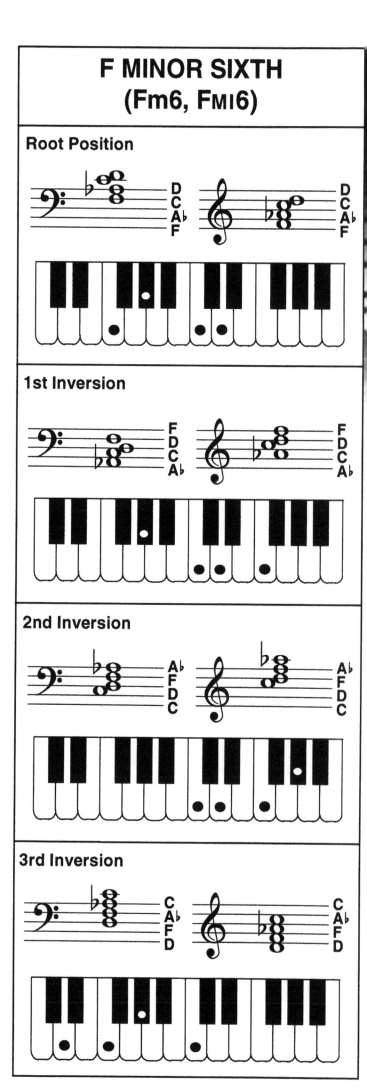

**Root Position**

**1st Inversion**

**2nd Inversion**

**3rd Inversion**

36

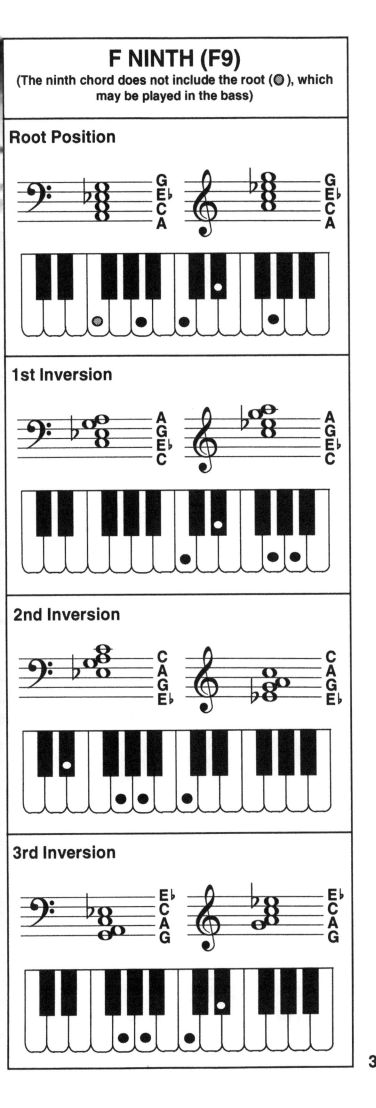

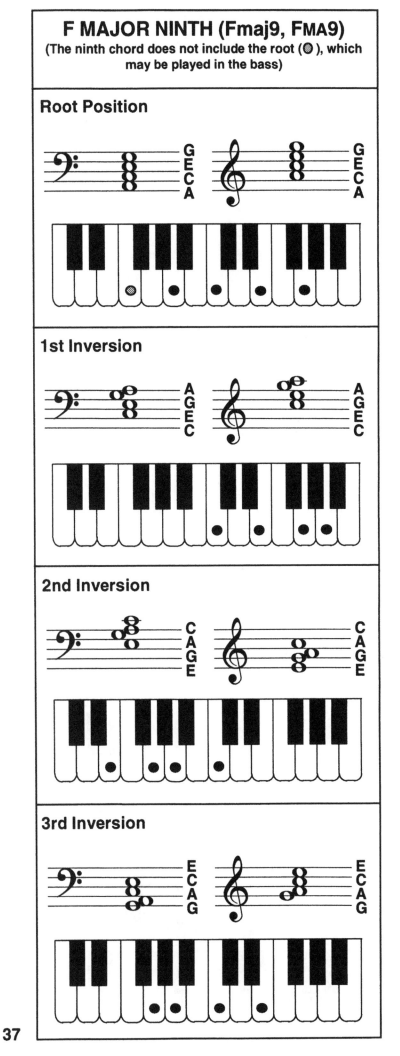

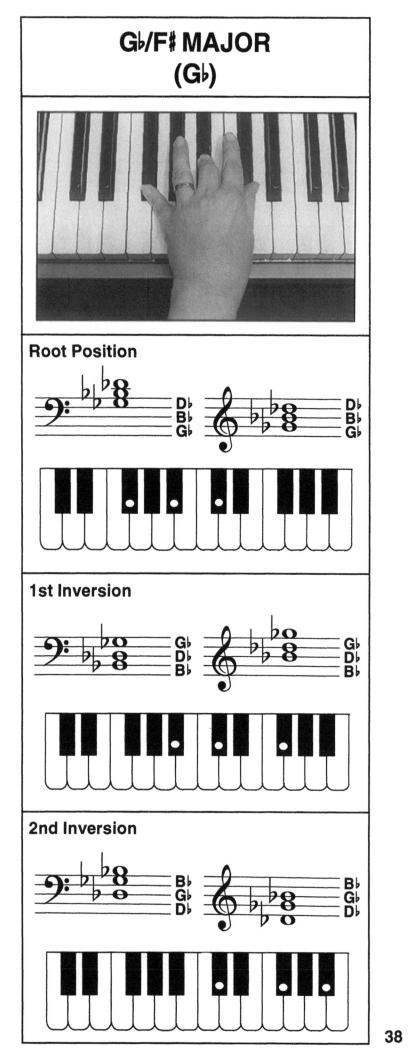

# Gb/F# MAJOR
## (Gb)

**Root Position**

Db
Bb
Gb

Db
Bb
Gb

**1st Inversion**

Gb
Db
Bb

Gb
Db
Bb

**2nd Inversion**

Bb
Gb
Db

Bb
Gb
Db

# F#/Gb MINOR
## (F#m)

**Root Position**

C#
A
F#

C#
A
F#

**1st Inversion**

F#
C#
A

F#
C#
A

**2nd Inversion**

A
F#
C#

A
F#
C#

38

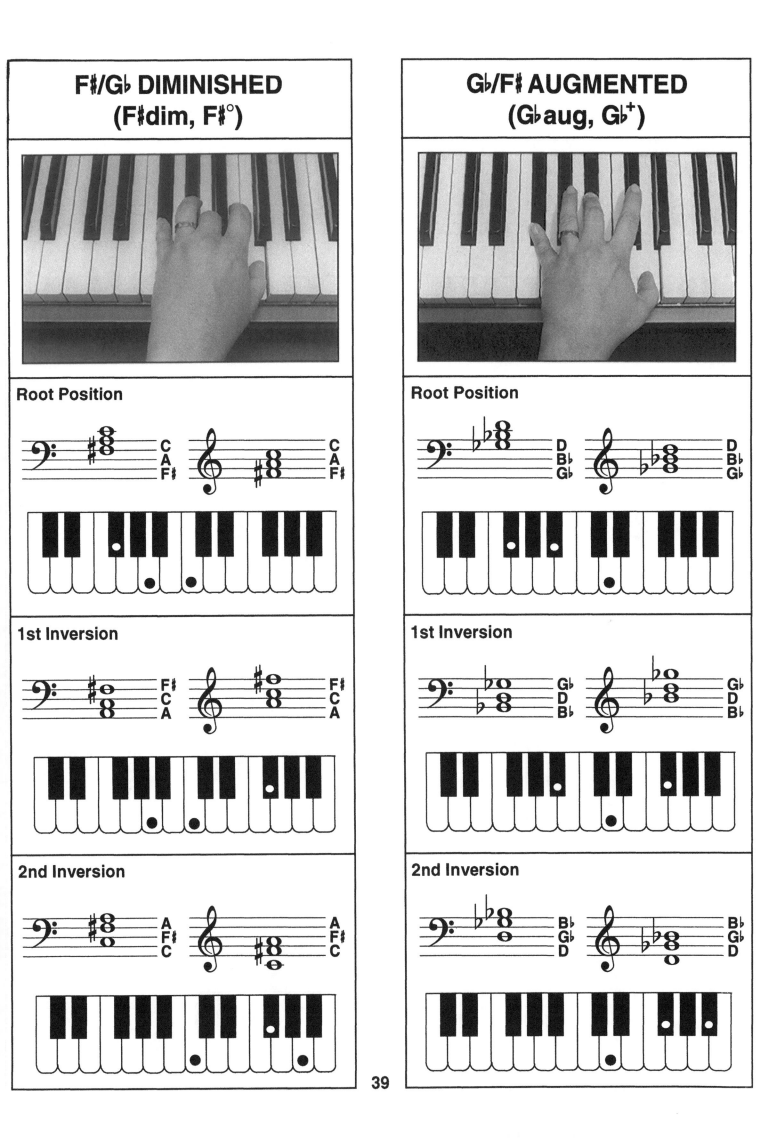

# F#/G♭ DIMINISHED
## (F#dim, F#°)

# G♭/F# AUGMENTED
## (G♭aug, G♭+)

**Root Position**

C
A
F#

C
A
F#

D
B♭
G♭

D
B♭
G♭

**1st Inversion**

F#
C
A

F#
C
A

G♭
D
B♭

G♭
D
B♭

**2nd Inversion**

A
F#
C

A
F#
C

B♭
G♭
D

B♭
G♭
D

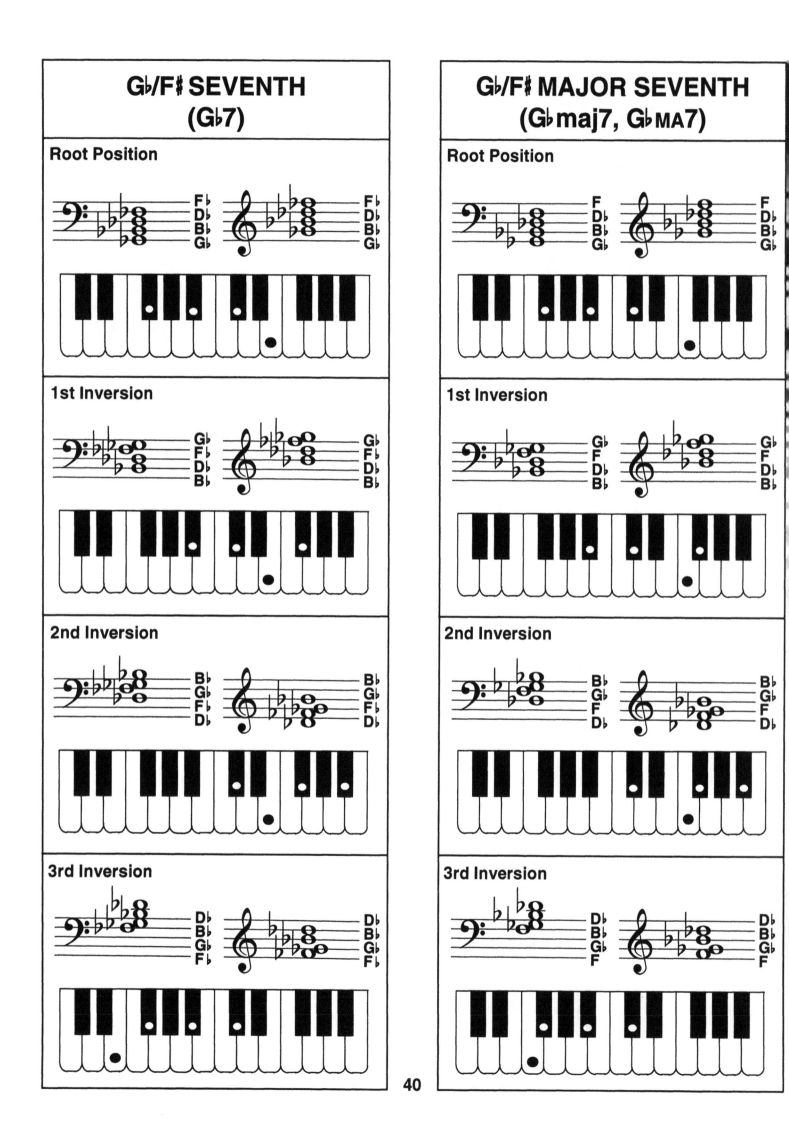

# F♯/G♭ MINOR SEVENTH
## (F♯m7, F♯MI7)

### Root Position

### 1st Inversion

### 2nd Inversion

### 3rd Inversion

# G♭/F♯ DIMINISHED SEVENTH
## (G♭dim7, G♭°7)

### Root Position          (Enharmonic Spelling)

### 1st Inversion

### 2nd Inversion

### 3rd Inversion

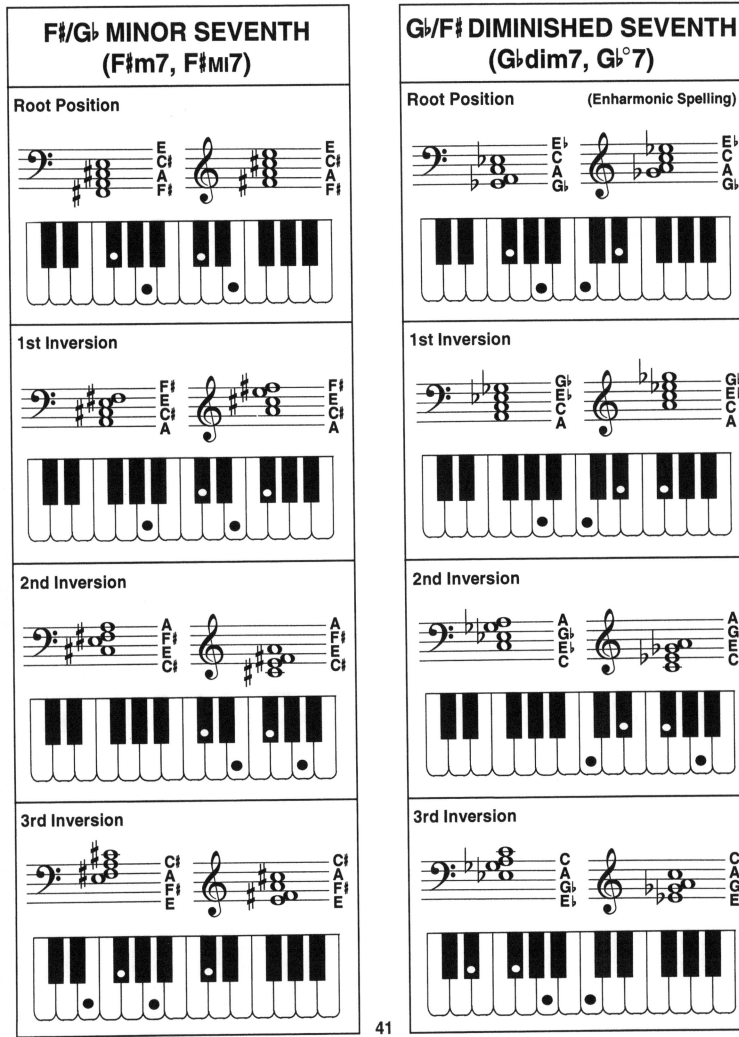

41

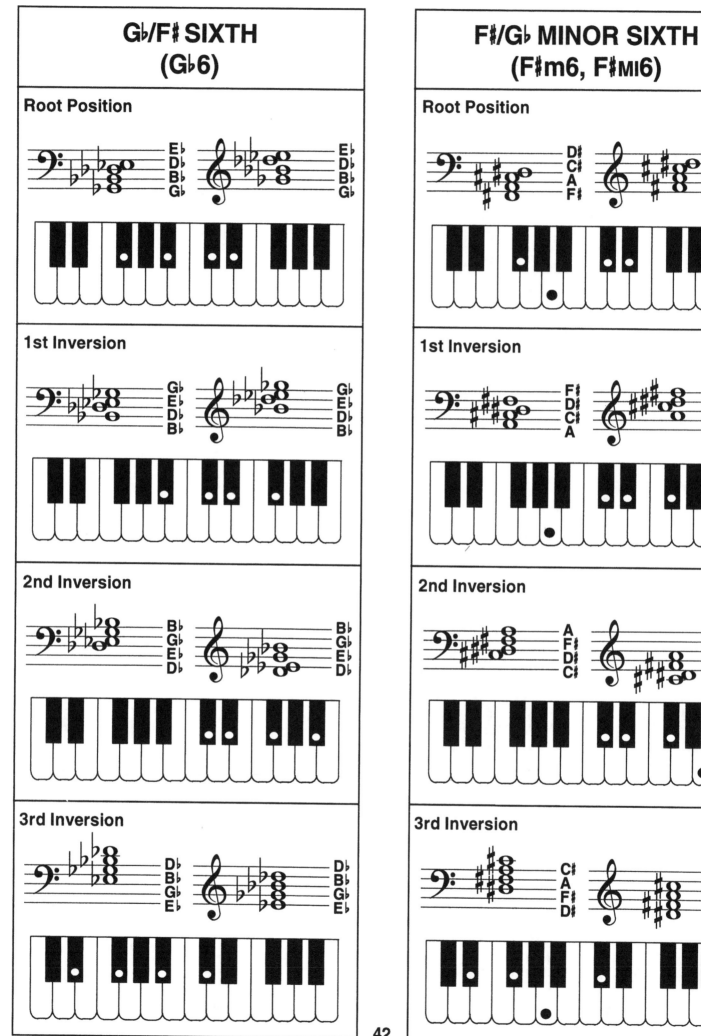

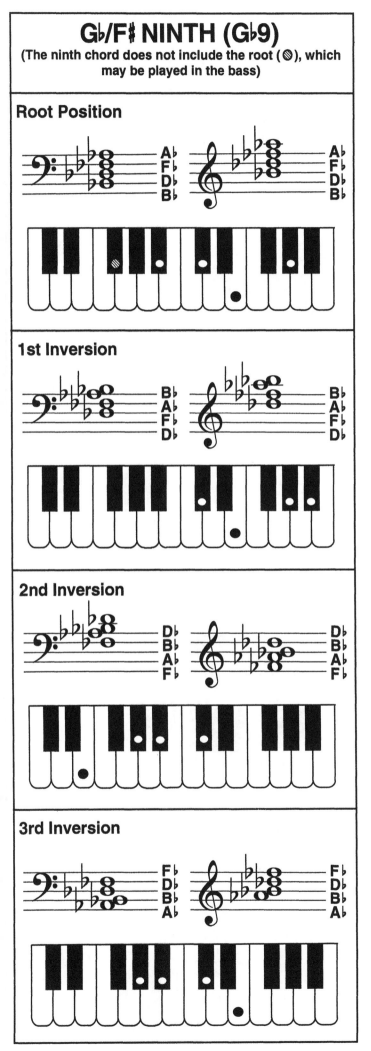

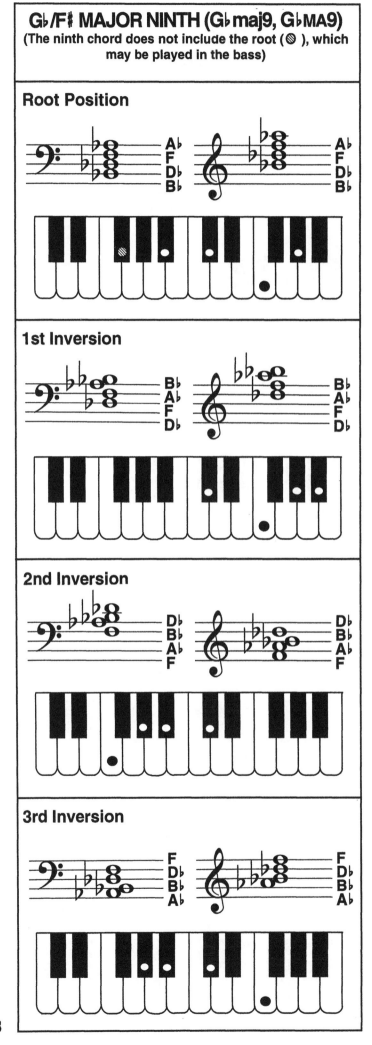

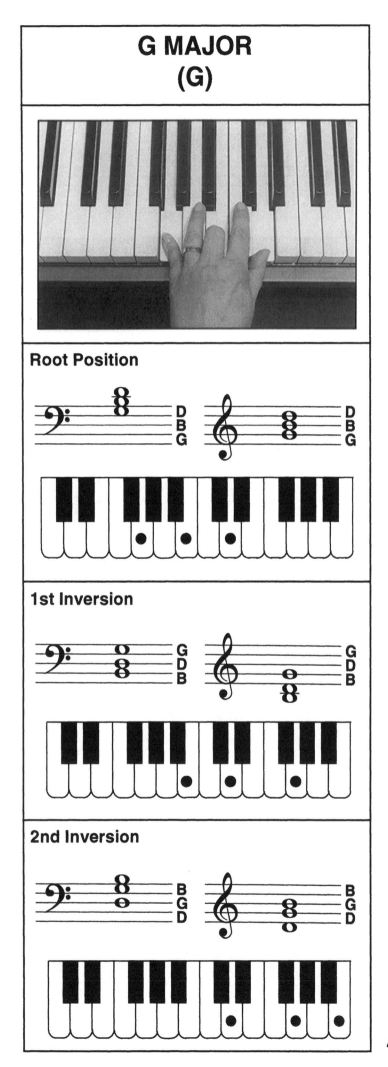

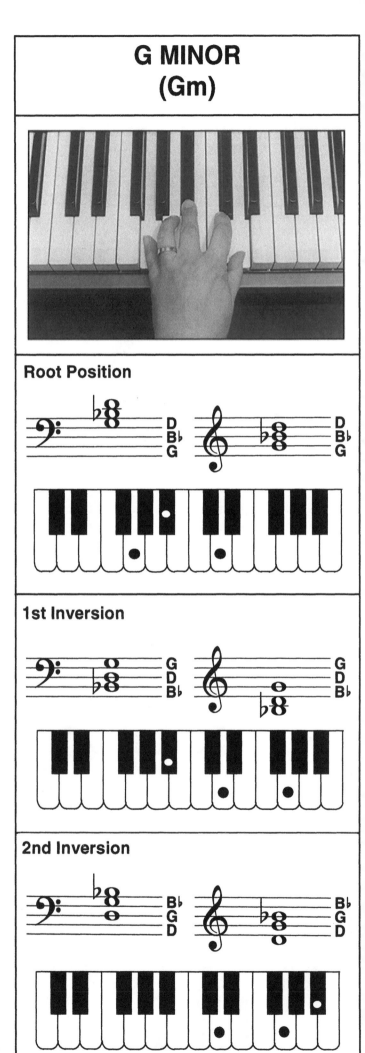

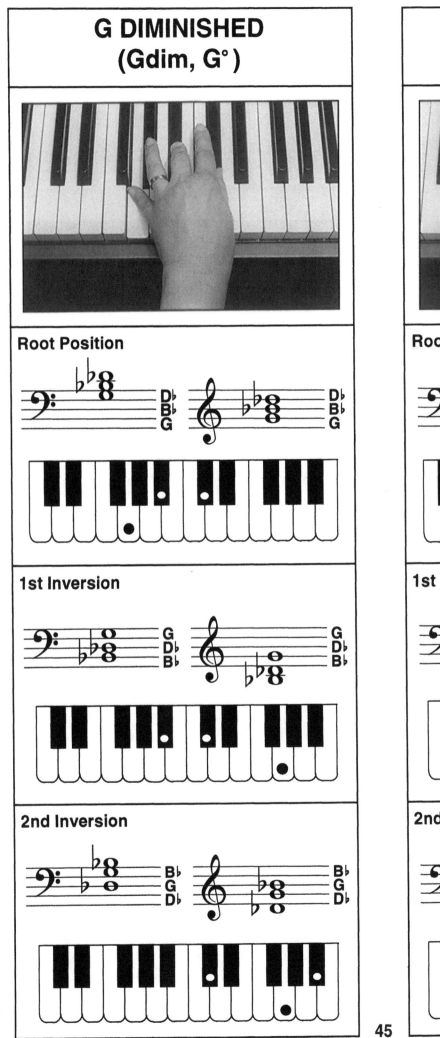

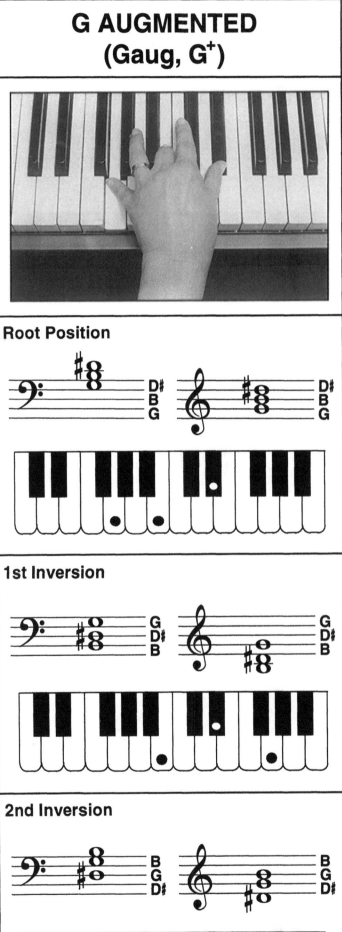

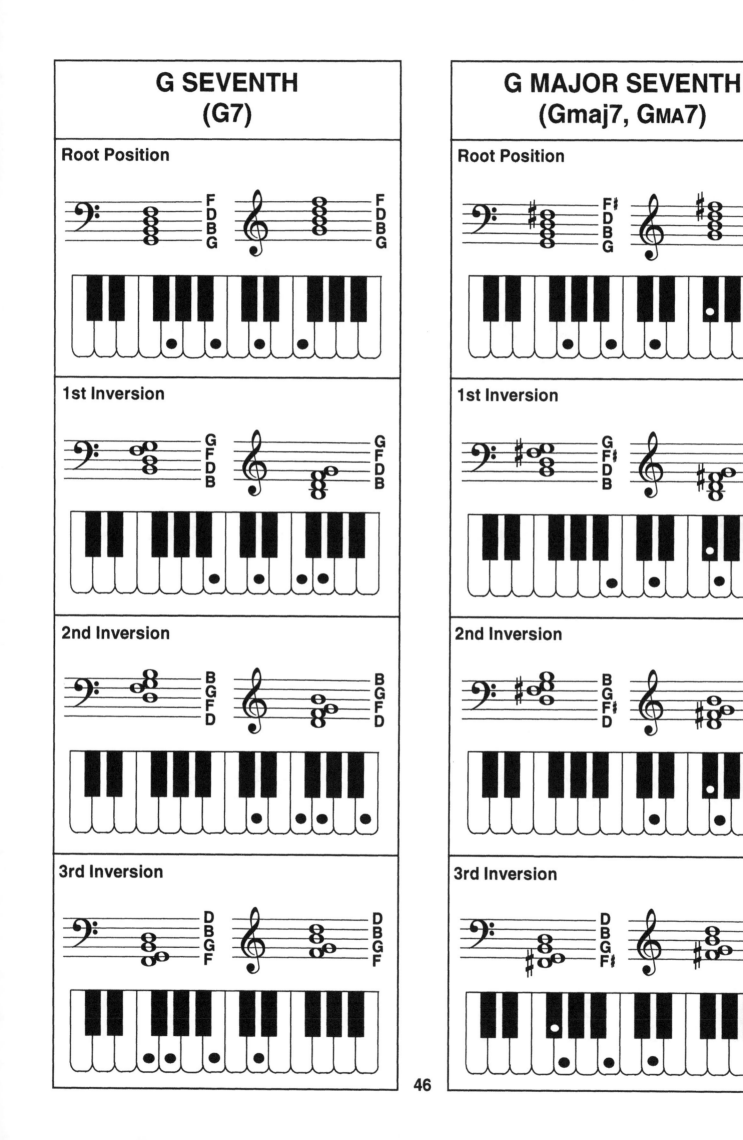

# G MINOR SEVENTH
## (Gm7, Gmi7)

### Root Position

### 1st Inversion

### 2nd Inversion

### 3rd Inversion

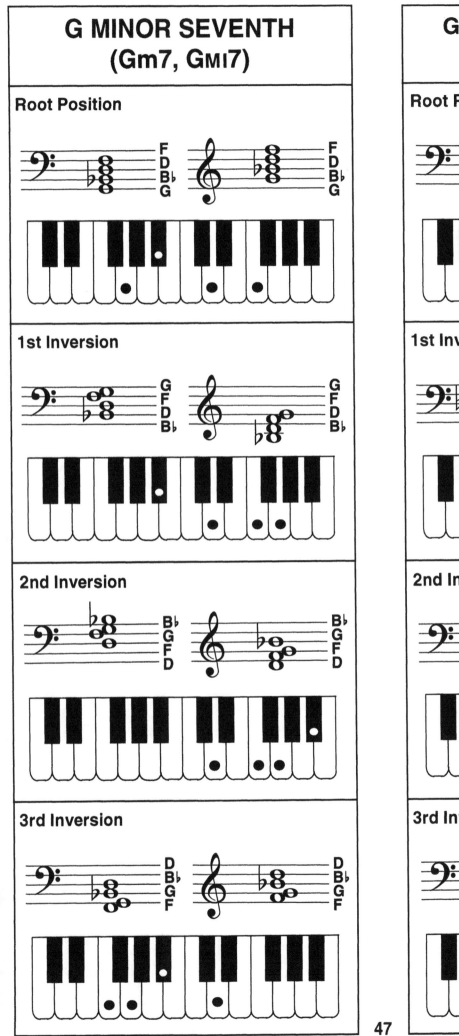

# G DIMINISHED SEVENTH
## (Gdim7, G°7)

### Root Position

### 1st Inversion

### 2nd Inversion

### 3rd Inversion

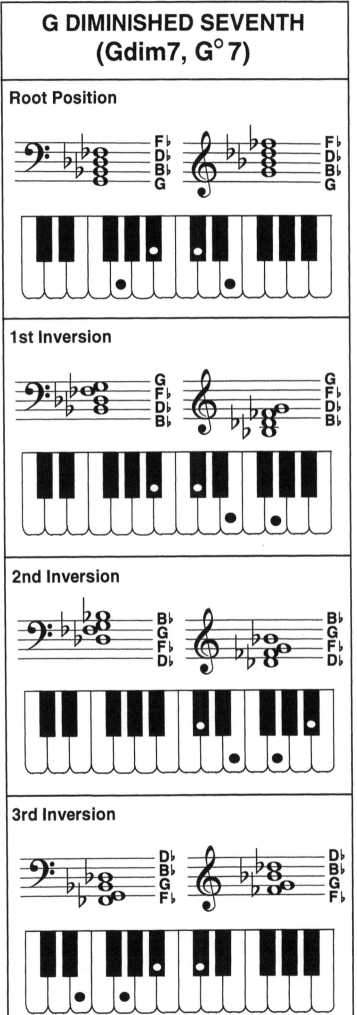

47

# G SIXTH
## (G6)

**Root Position**

**1st Inversion**

**2nd Inversion**

**3rd Inversion**

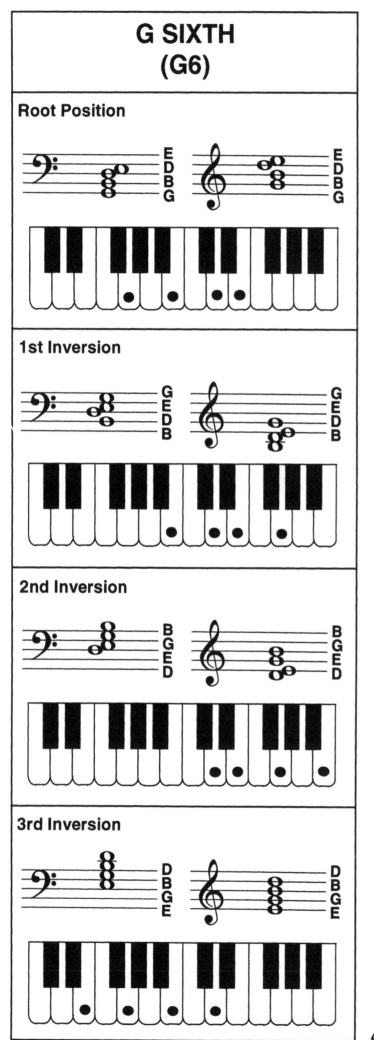

# G MINOR SIXTH
## (Gm6, Gmi6)

**Root Position**

**1st Inversion**

**2nd Inversion**

**3rd Inversion**

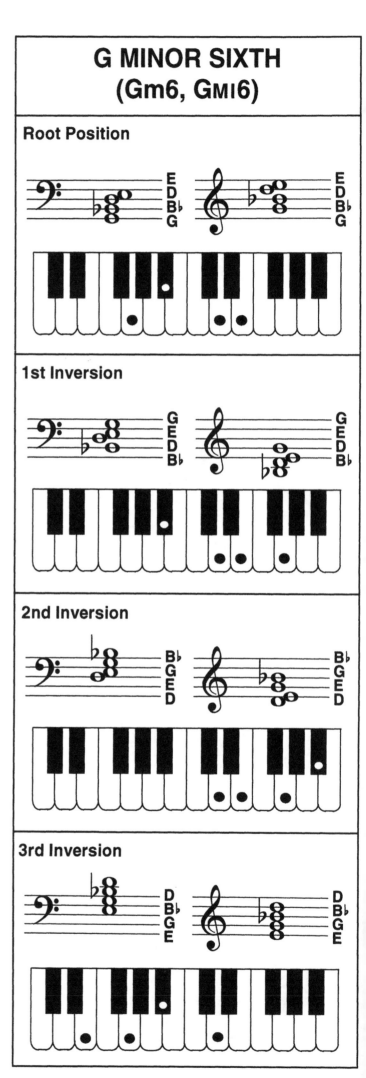

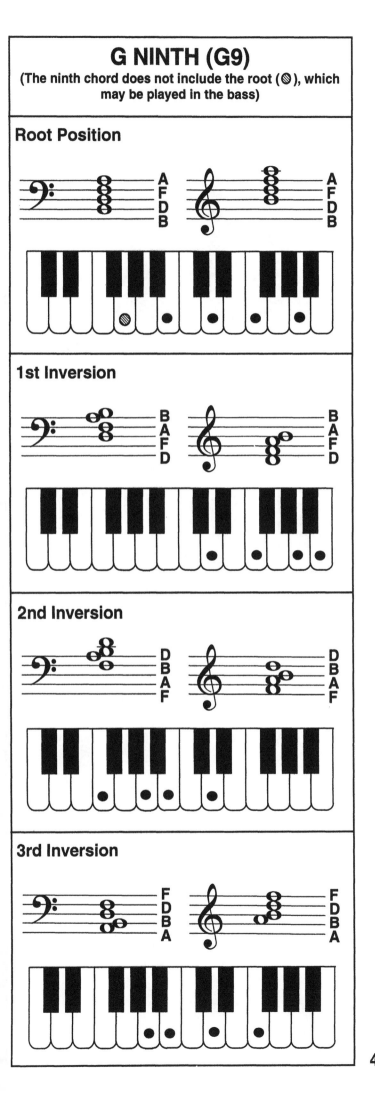
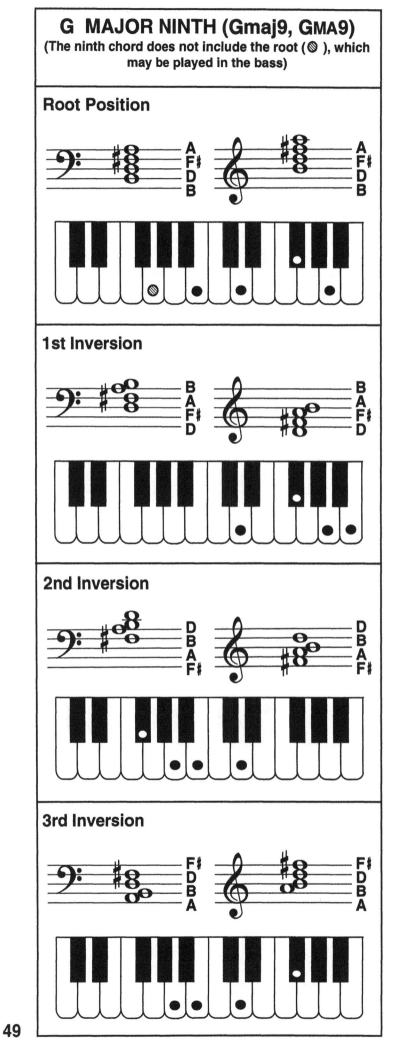

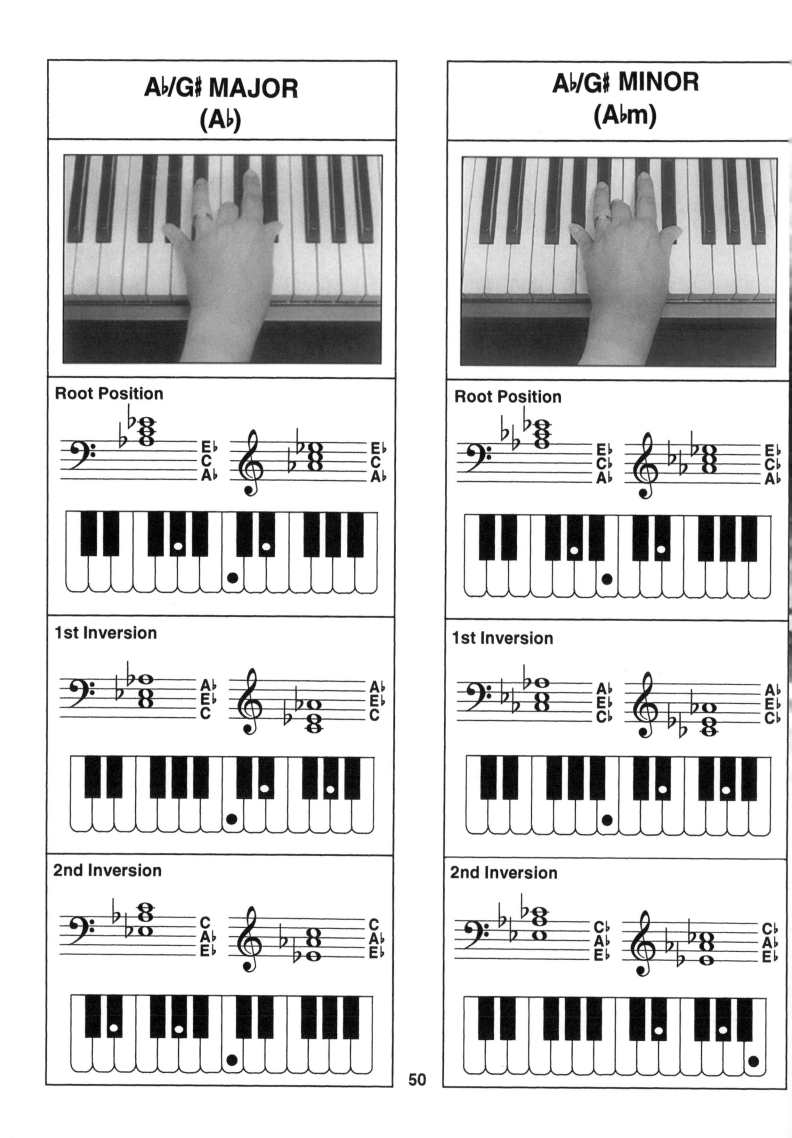

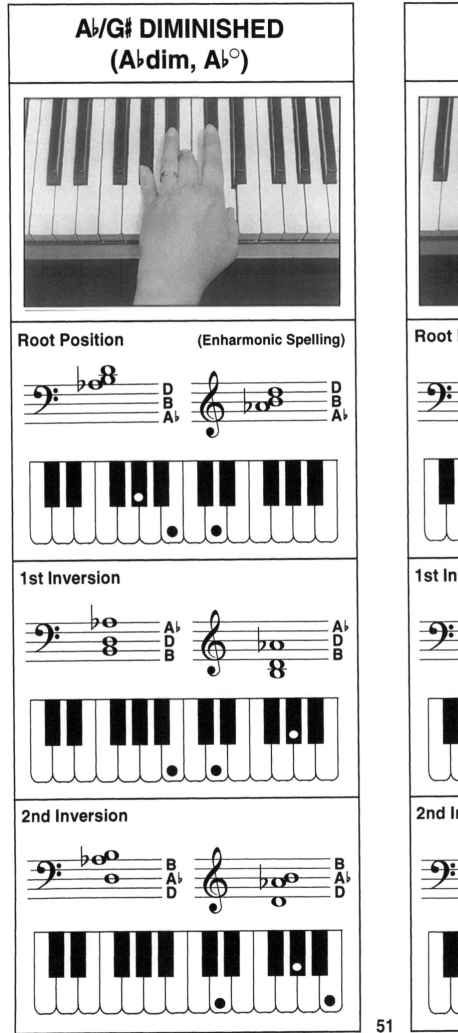

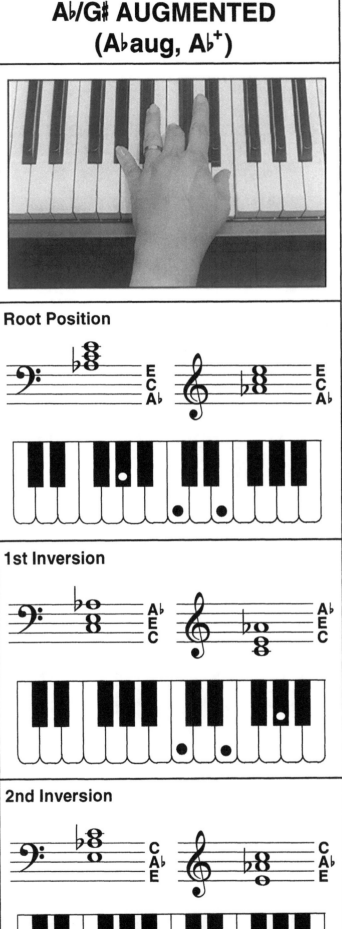

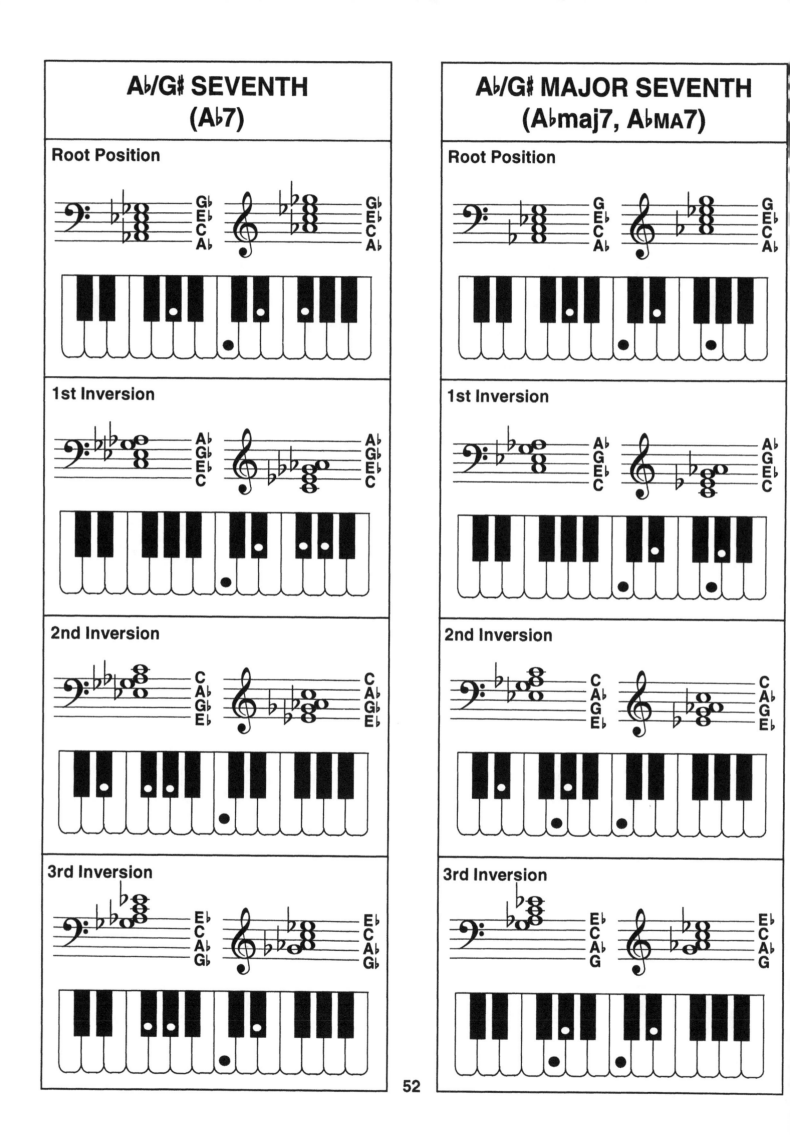

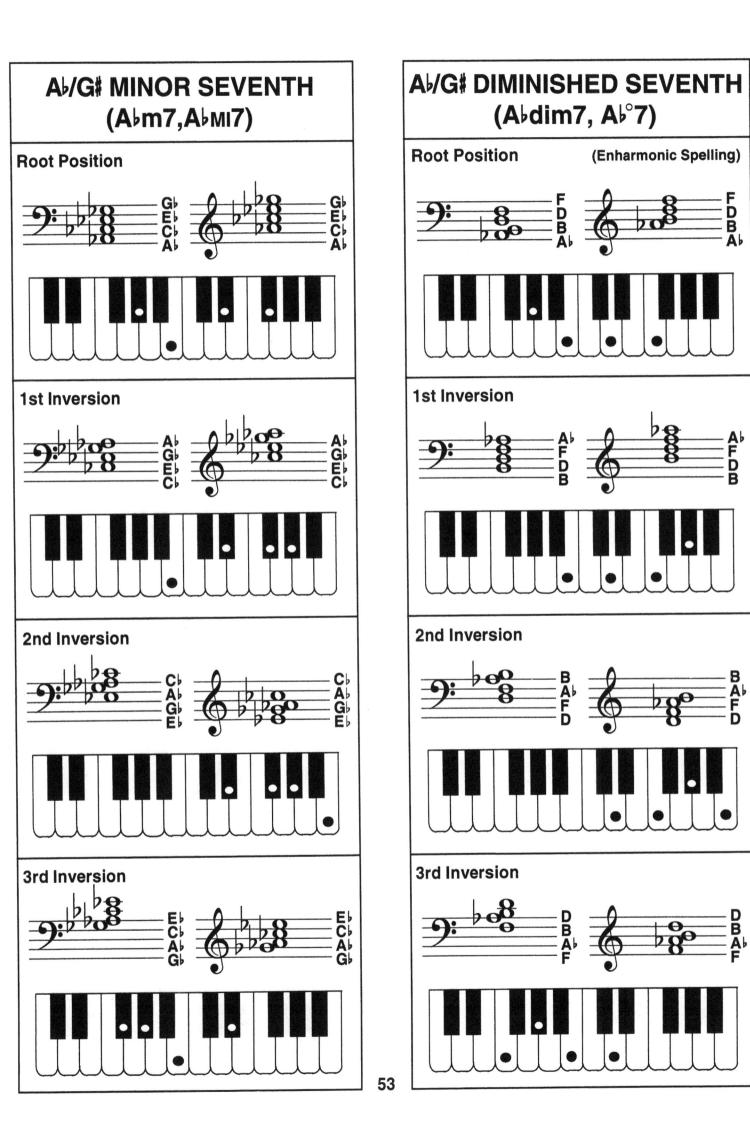

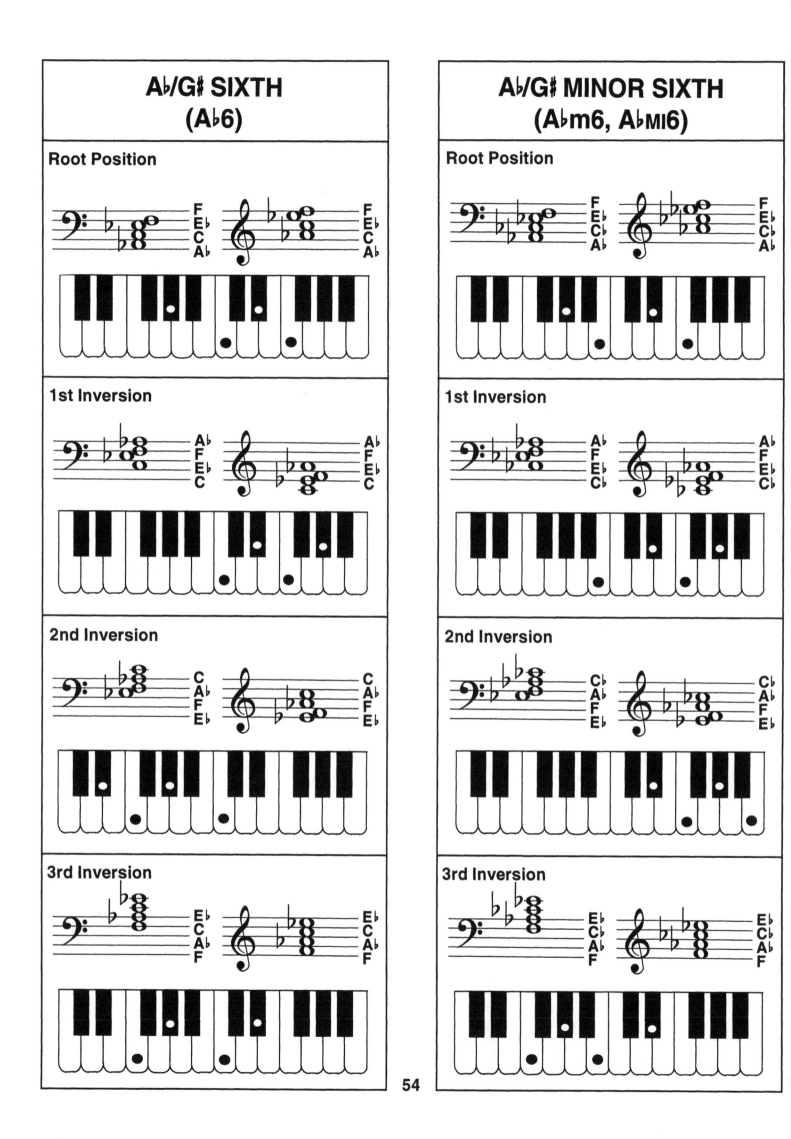

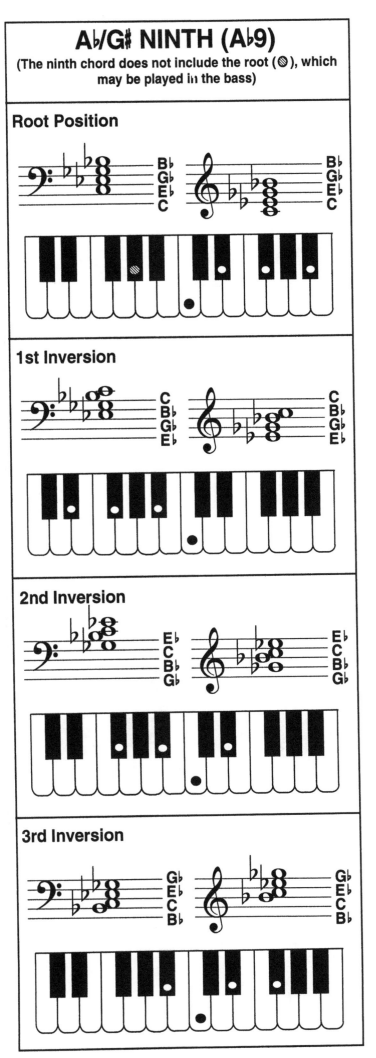

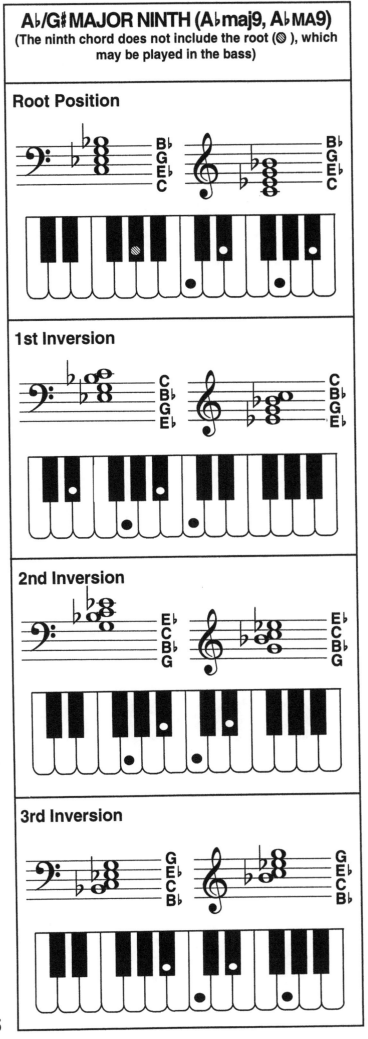

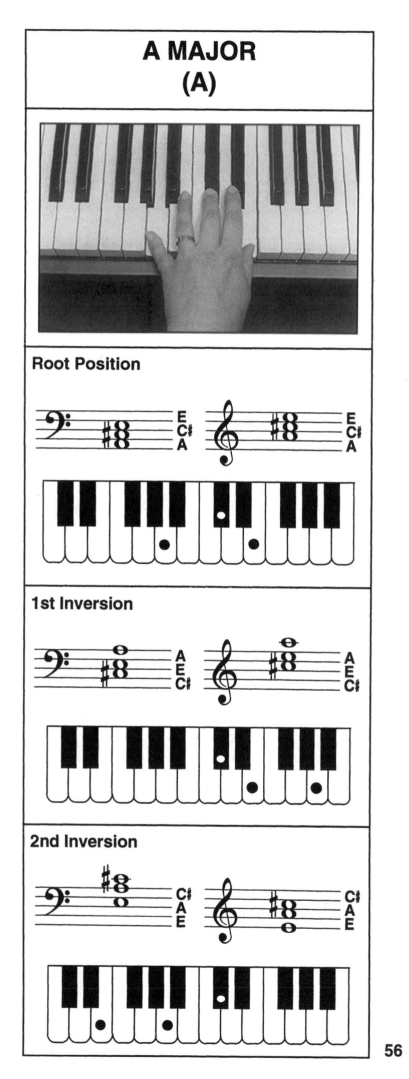
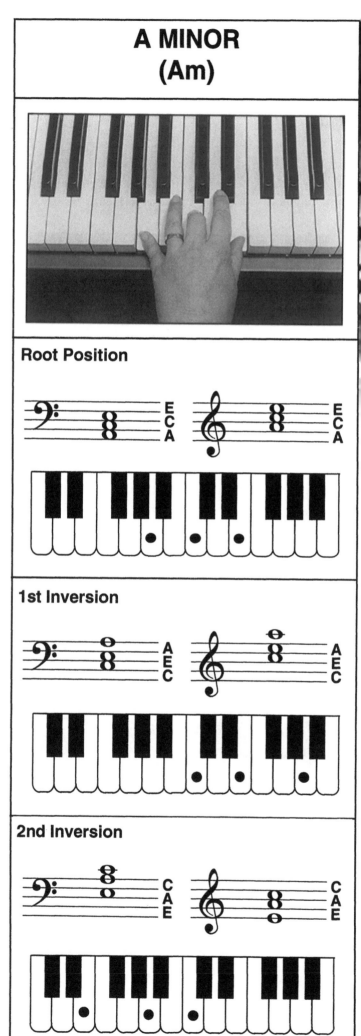

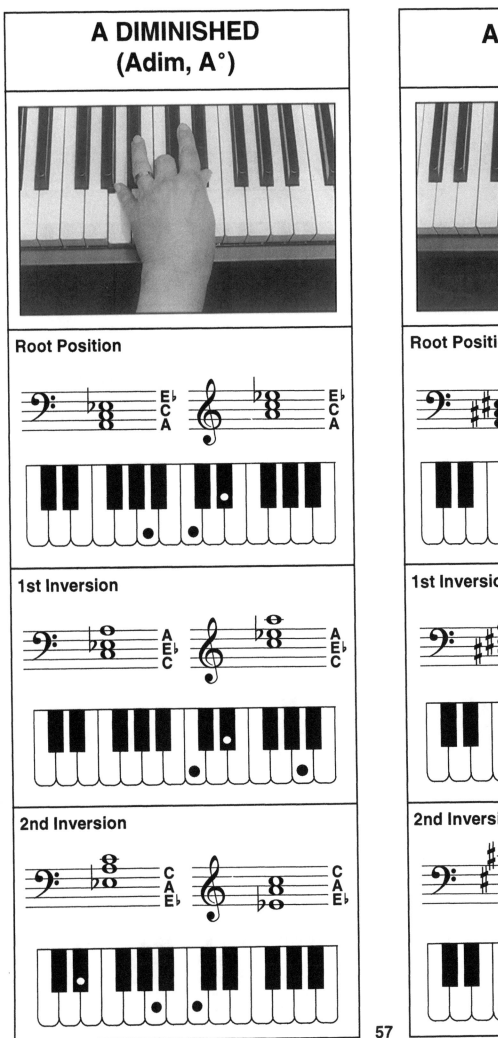

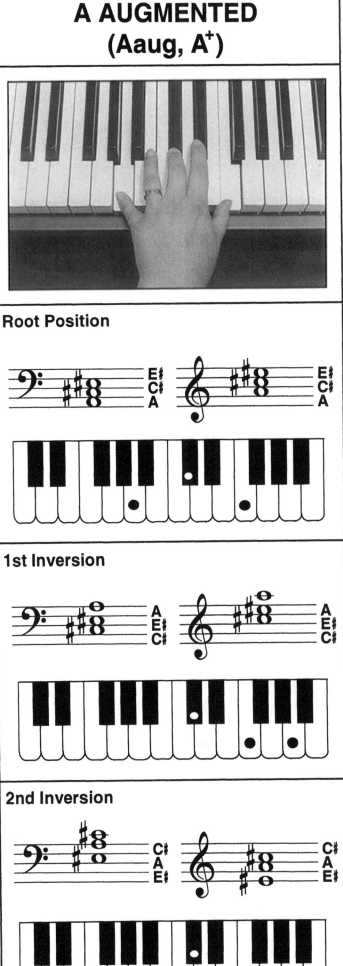

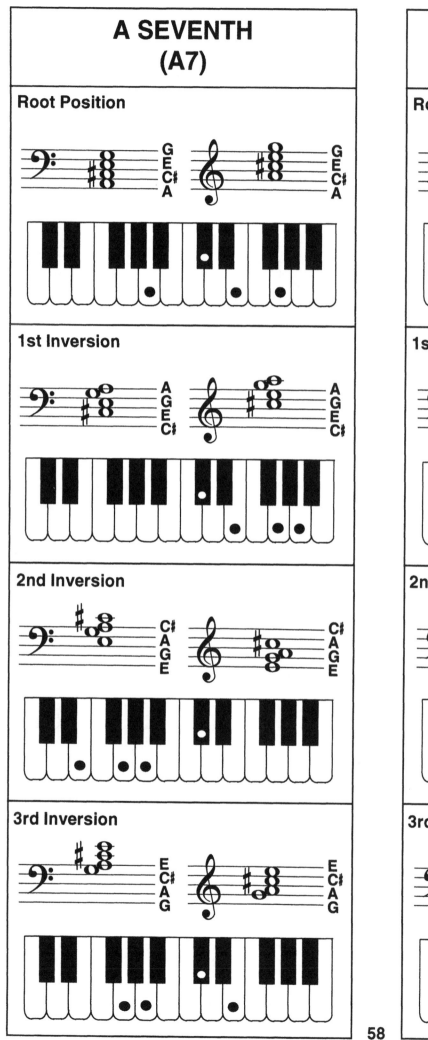

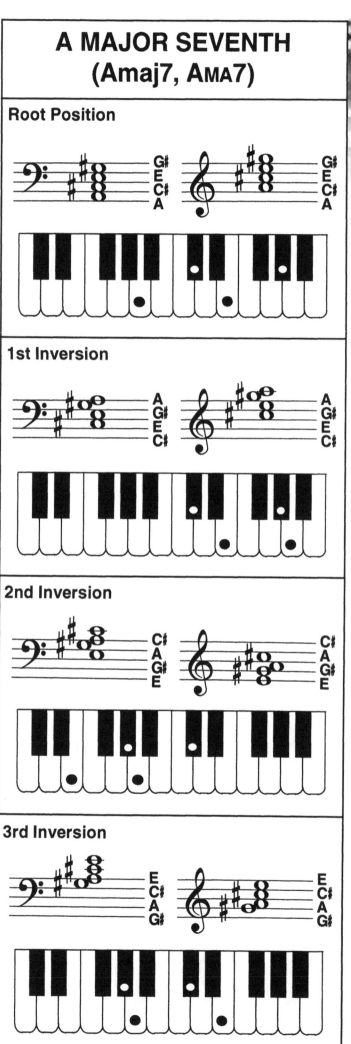

58

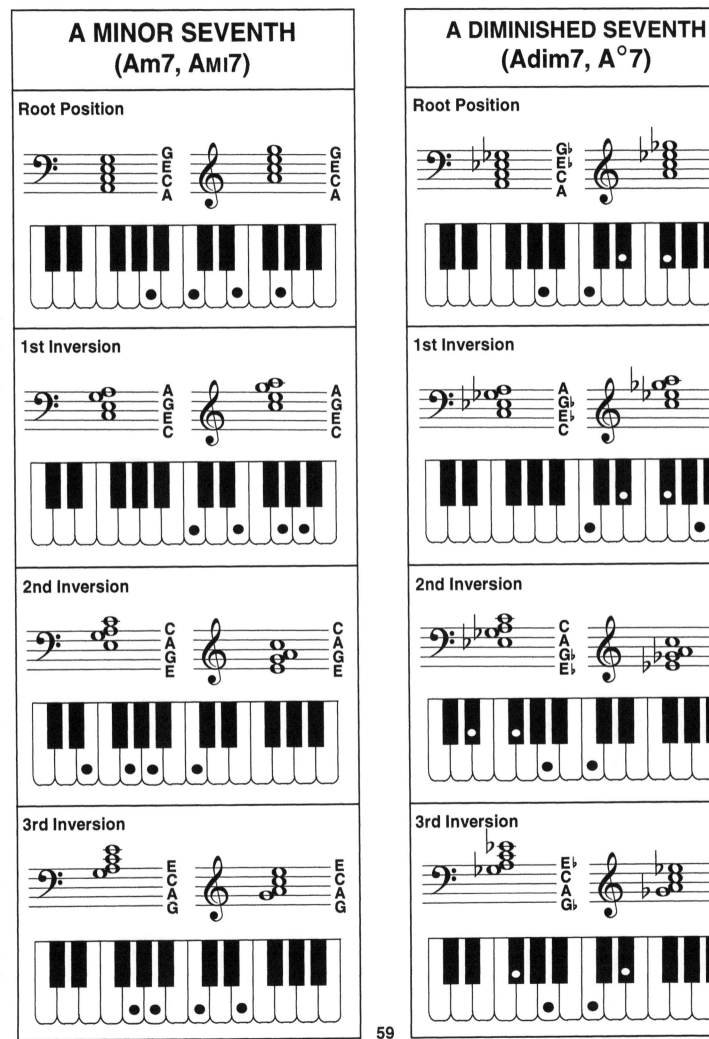

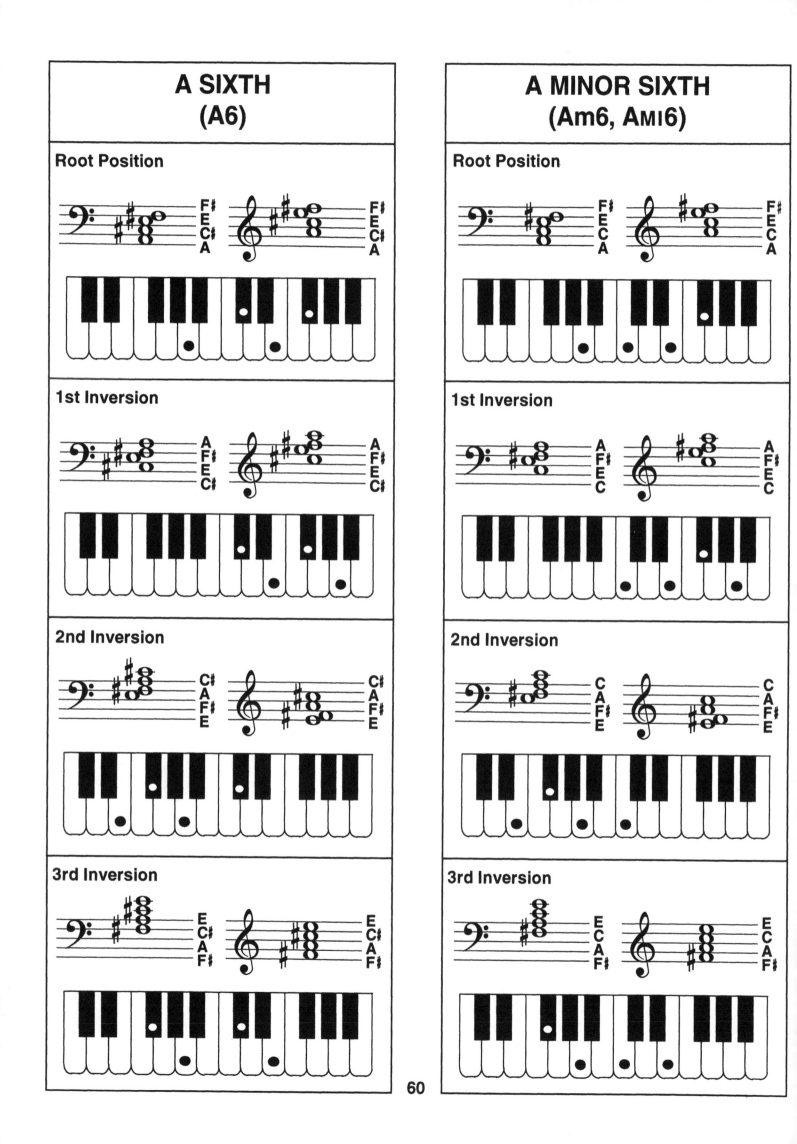

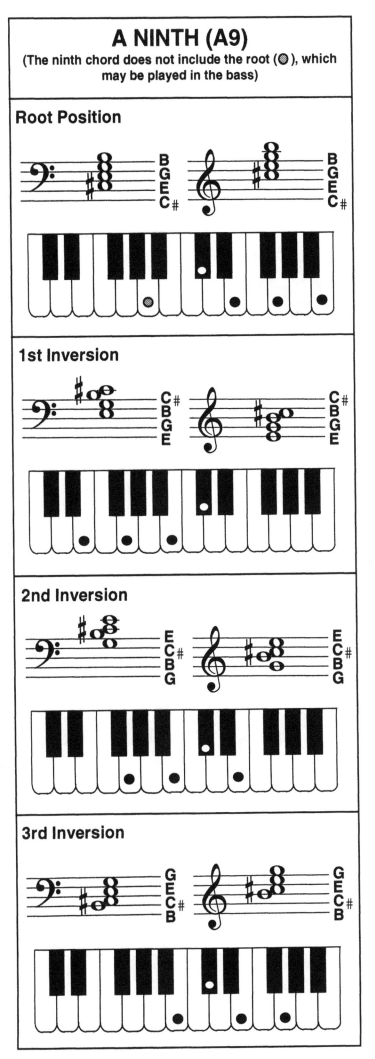

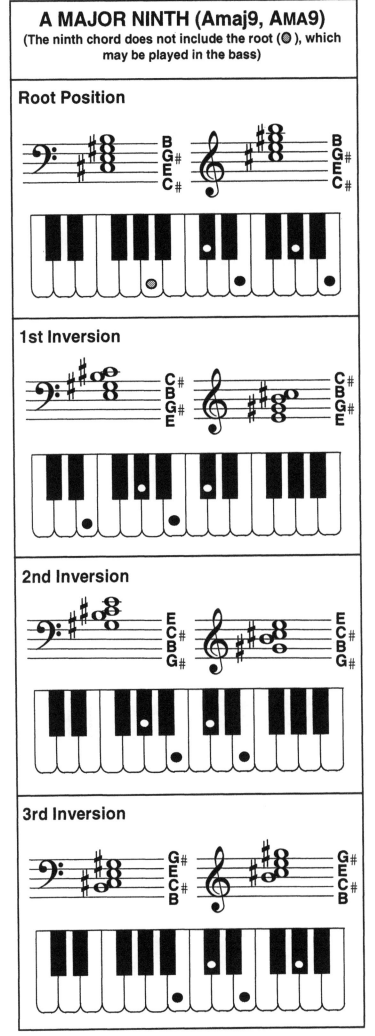

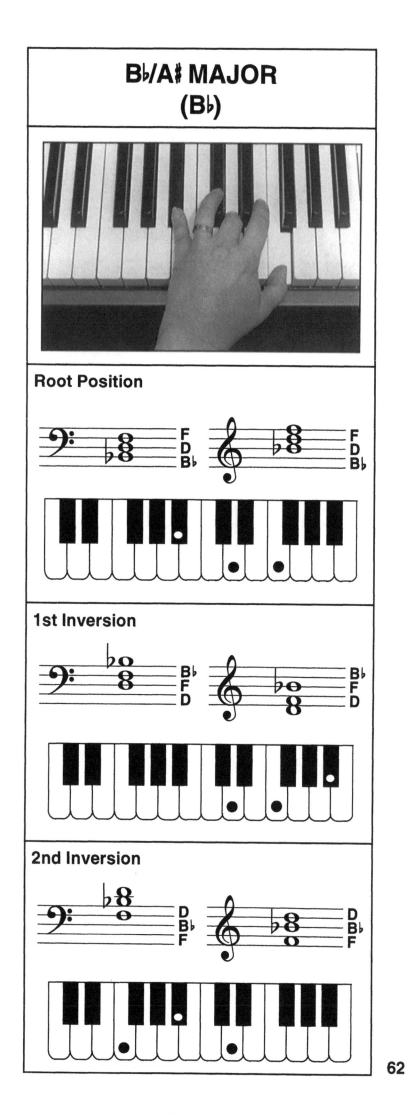

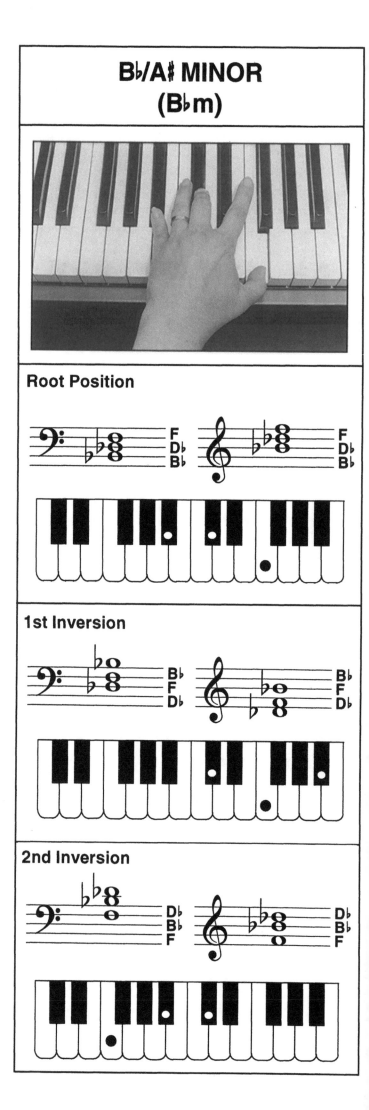

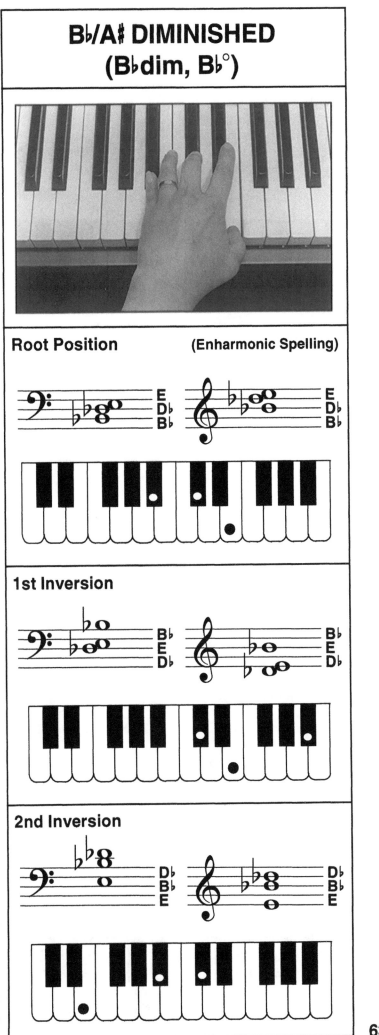
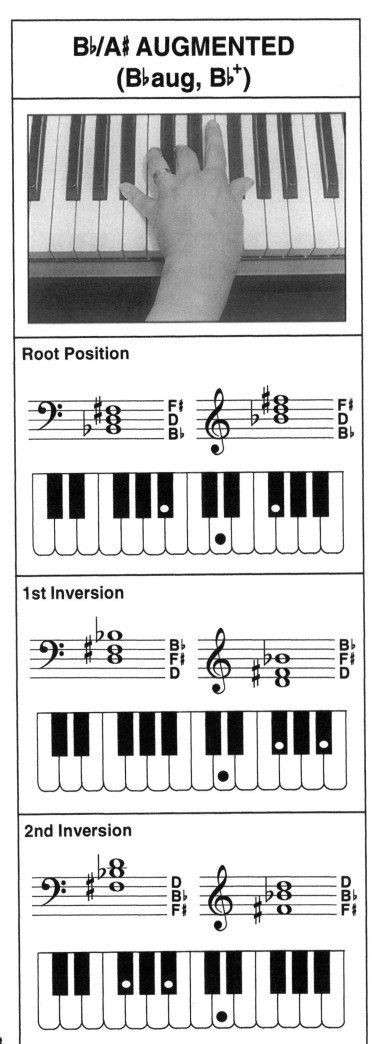

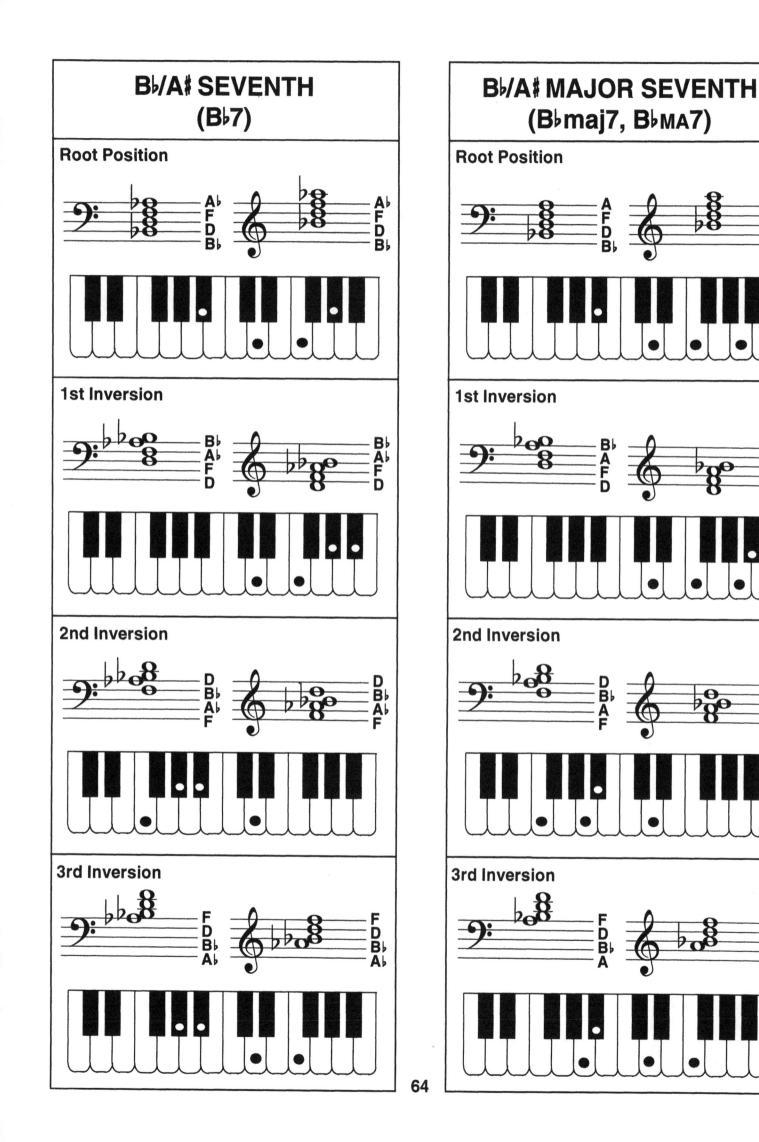

# B♭/A♯ MINOR SEVENTH
## (B♭m7, B♭MI7)

### Root Position

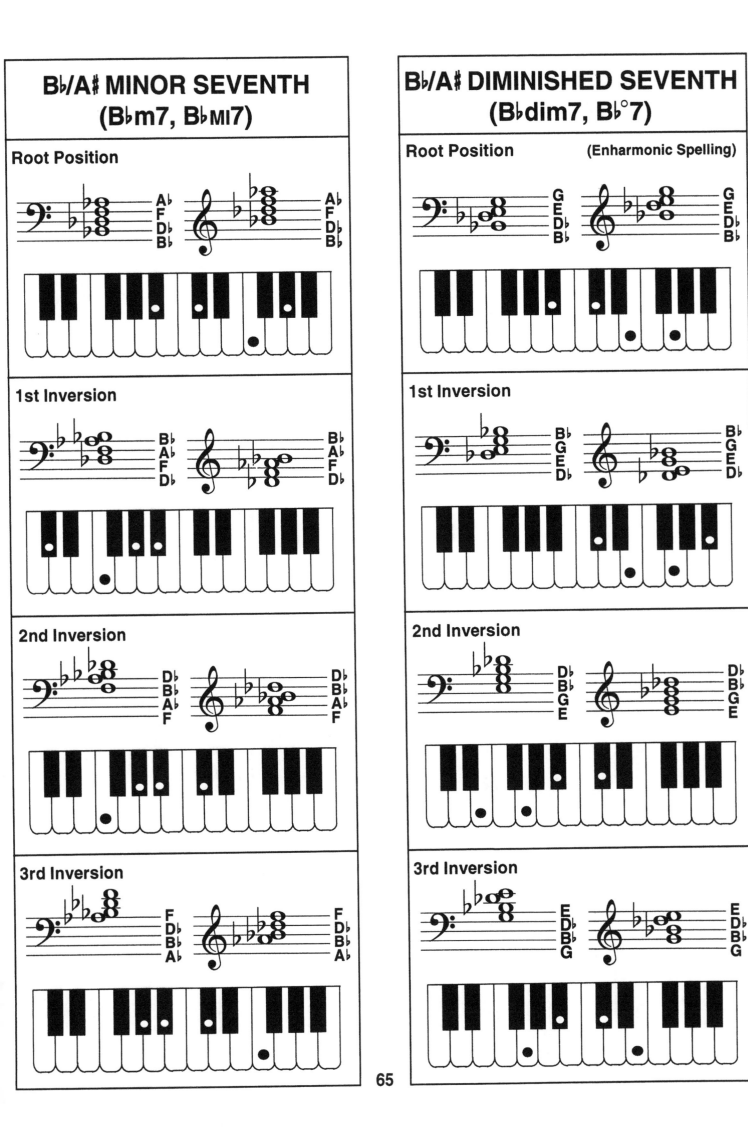

| | A♭ |
|---|---|
| | F |
| | D♭ |
| | B♭ |

### 1st Inversion

| | B♭ |
|---|---|
| | A♭ |
| | F |
| | D♭ |

### 2nd Inversion

| | D♭ |
|---|---|
| | B♭ |
| | A♭ |
| | F |

### 3rd Inversion

| | F |
|---|---|
| | D♭ |
| | B♭ |
| | A♭ |

# B♭/A♯ DIMINISHED SEVENTH
## (B♭dim7, B♭°7)

### Root Position     (Enharmonic Spelling)

| | G |
|---|---|
| | E |
| | D♭ |
| | B♭ |

### 1st Inversion

| | B♭ |
|---|---|
| | G |
| | E |
| | D♭ |

### 2nd Inversion

| | D♭ |
|---|---|
| | B |
| | G |
| | E |

### 3rd Inversion

| | E |
|---|---|
| | D♭ |
| | B♭ |
| | G |

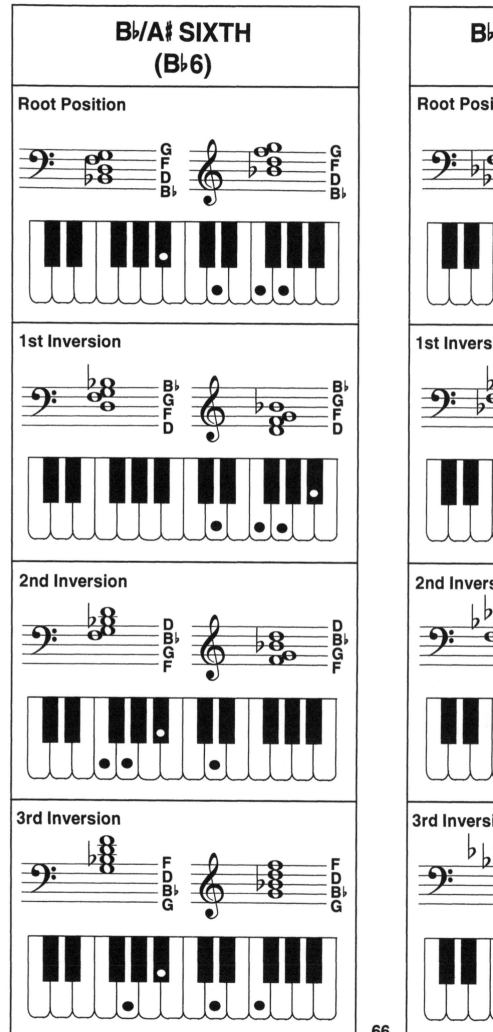

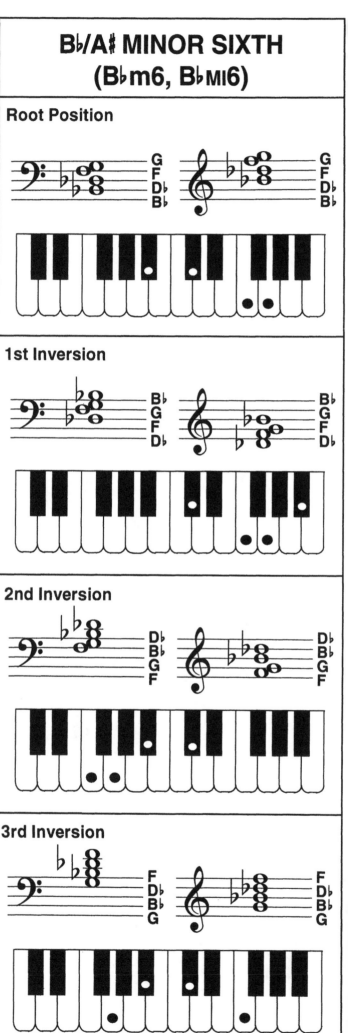

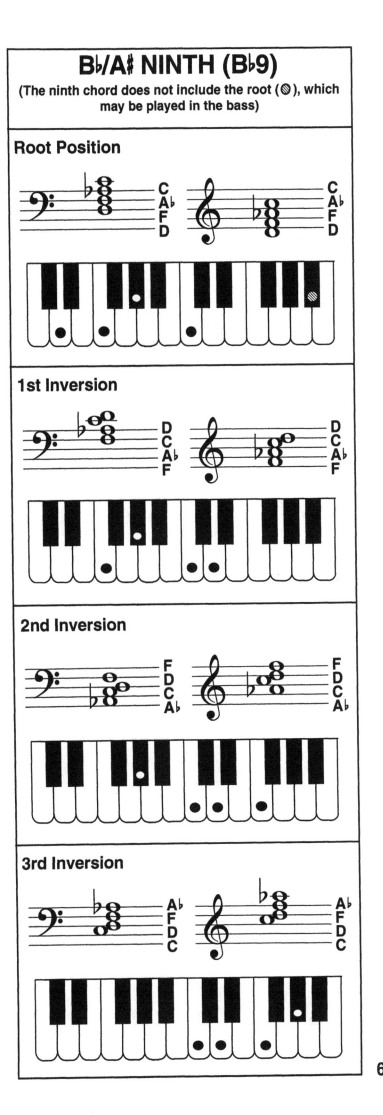

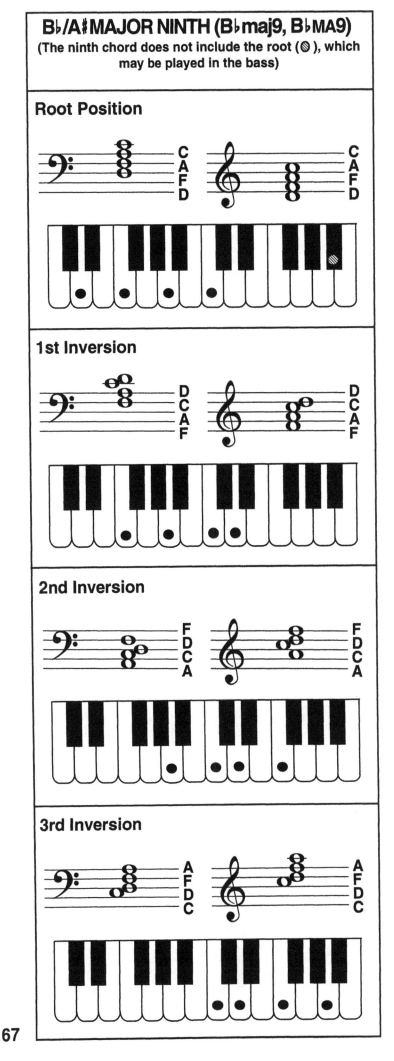

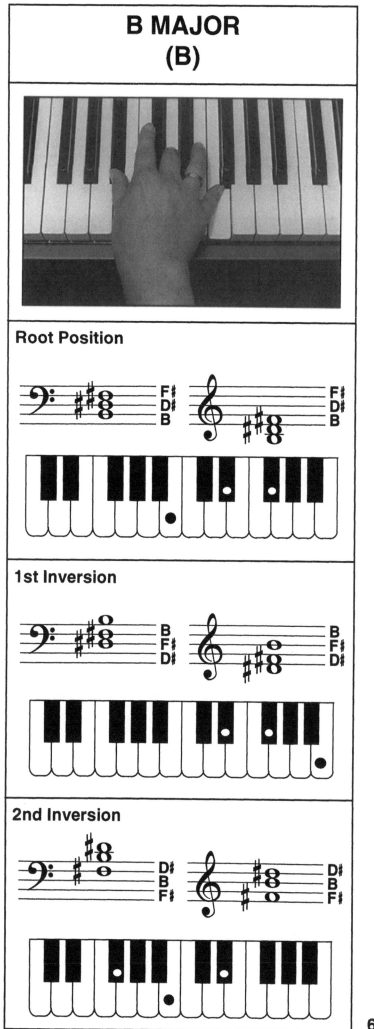

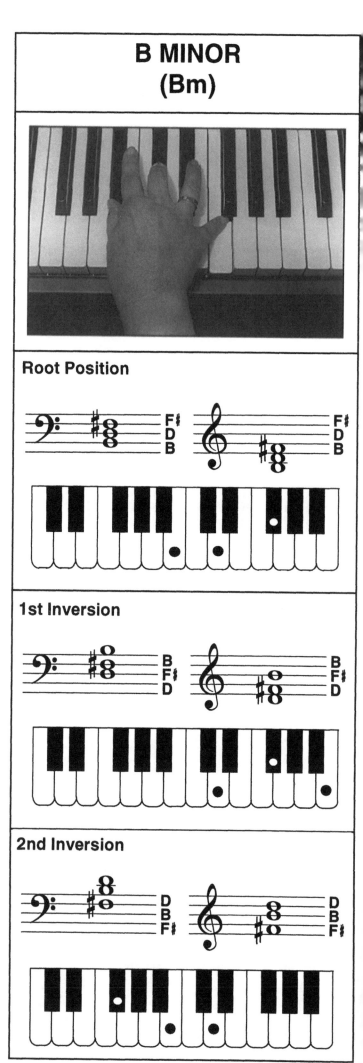

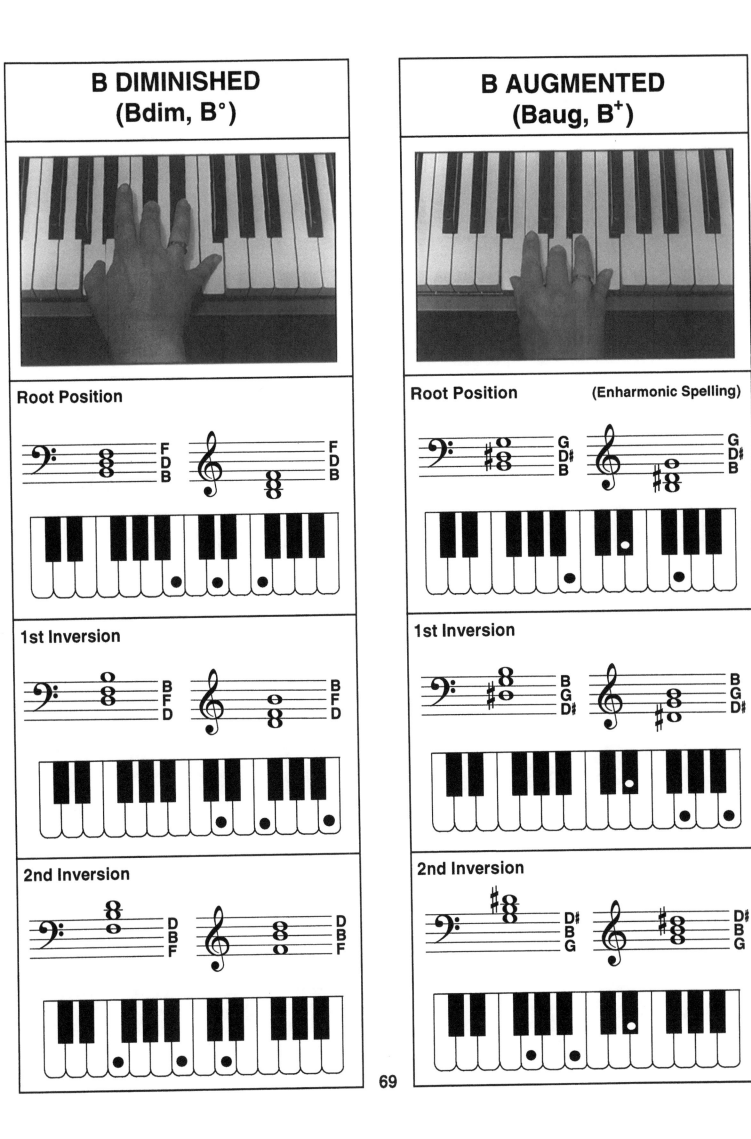

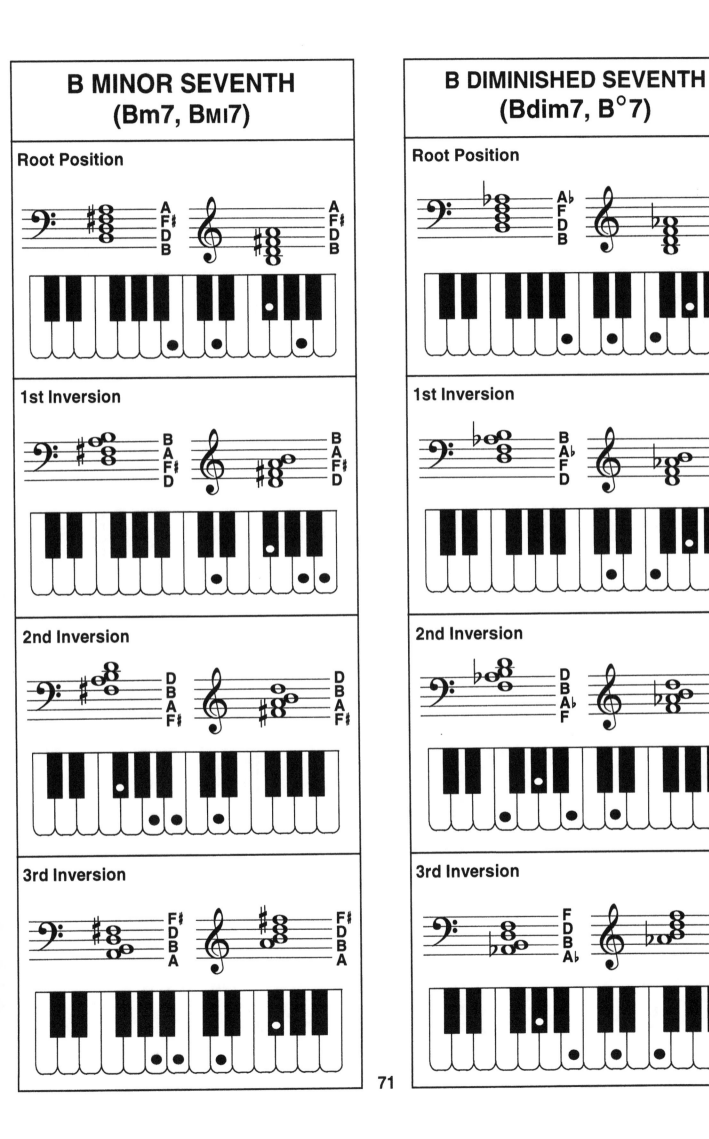

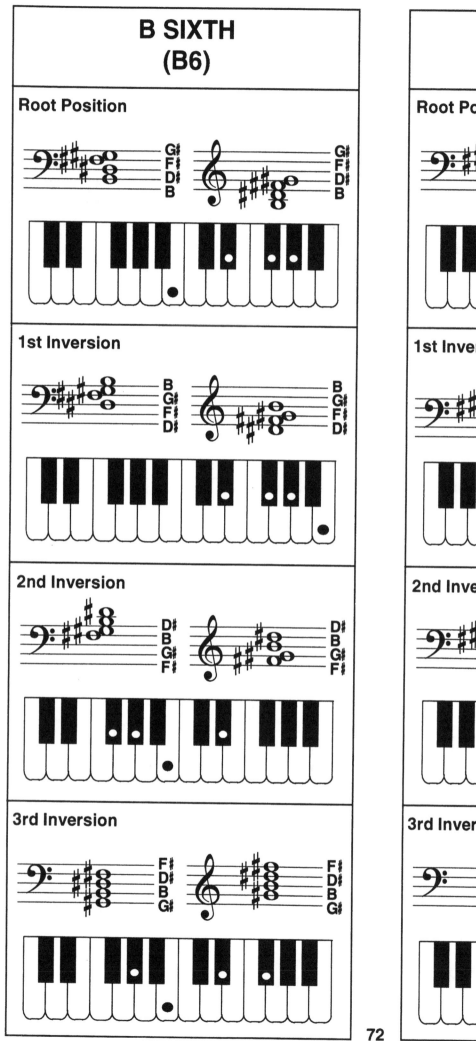

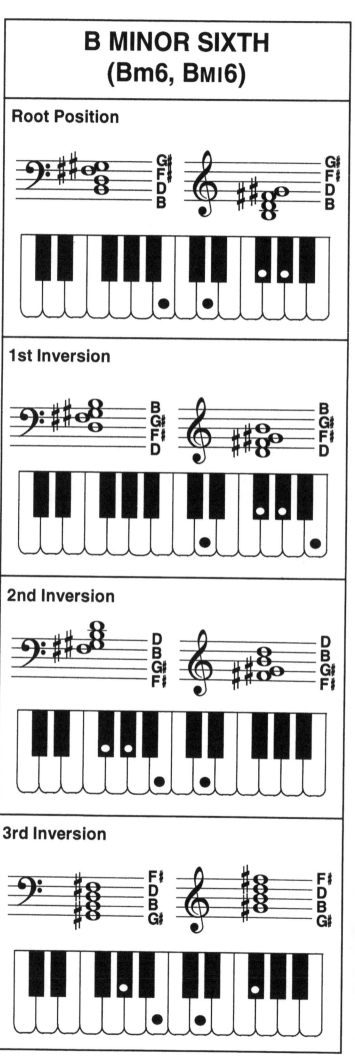

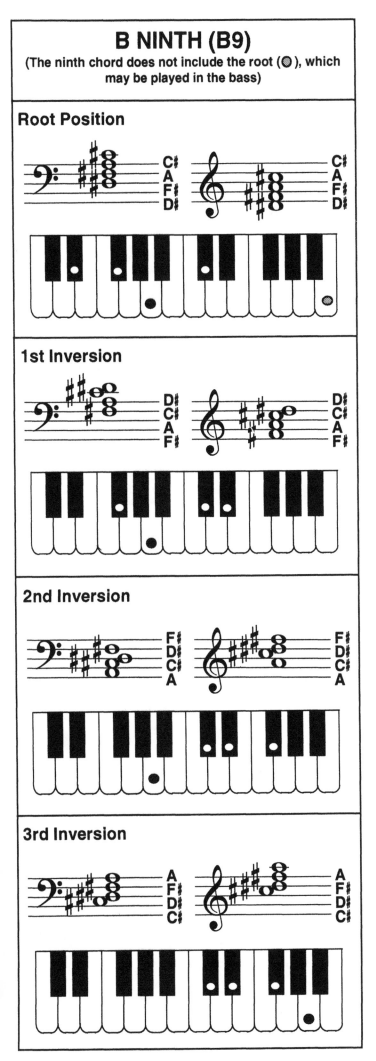

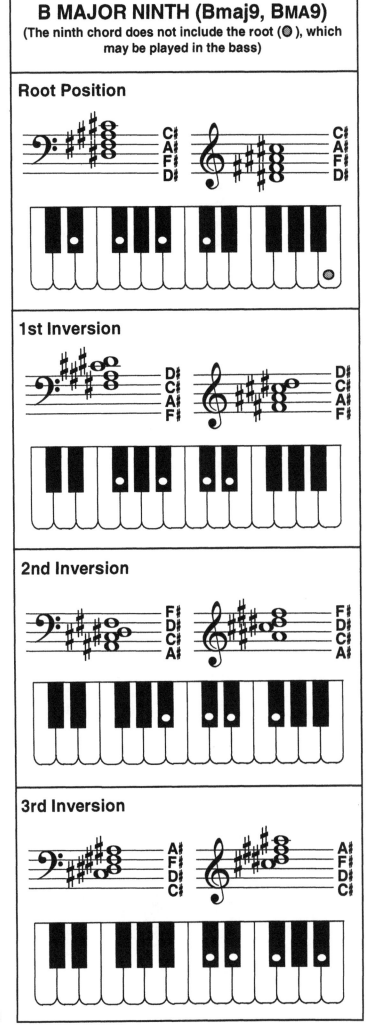

# CHORD CONSTRUCTION

## Chords can be built either of two ways:

Method 1: Using the degree (or number) on the scale of the notes

For example, the C chord made up of C, E, and G is 1, 3, 5. This is because C is the first note in the C scale, E the third, and G the fifth.

Method 2: Stacking up intervals of thirds

An interval is the distance between two notes. For example, the distance between C and E is an interval of a third, because C and E are three letter names apart.

C and E is called a major third because E is 4 half steps (semitones) up from C.

C and Eb is called a minor third because Eb is only 3 half steps (semitones) up from C.

## Four Basic Triads

The four basic triads (3-note chords) that all other chords are built on may be expressed by either Method 1 or Method 2 above.

Major triad = 1, 3, 5 (Method 1), or a major 3rd + a minor 3rd (Method 2).
    For example, in the key of C (C E G)
*   a major 3rd (or 4 half steps) up from C is E
*   a minor 3rd (or 3 half steps) up from E is G

Minor triad = 1, 3L, 5 (L means to the left or lower by a half step), or a minor 3rd + a major 3rd.
    For example, in the key of C (C Eb G)
*   a minor 3rd (or 3 half steps) up from C is E flat
*   a major 3rd (or 4 half steps) up from E flat is G

Diminished triad = 1, 3L, 5L, or a minor 3rd + a minor 3rd.
    For example, in the key of C (C E Gb)
*   a minor 3rd (or 3 half steps) up from C is E flat
*   a minor 3rd (or 3 half steps) up from E is Gb flat

Augmented triad = 1, 3, 5R (R means to the right or raise by a half step), or
                a major 3rd + a major 3rd.
    For example, in the key of C (C E G#)
*   a major 3rd (or 4 half steps) up from C is E
*   a major 3rd (or 4 half steps) up from E is G#

# FOUR BASIC TRIADS

**Major**

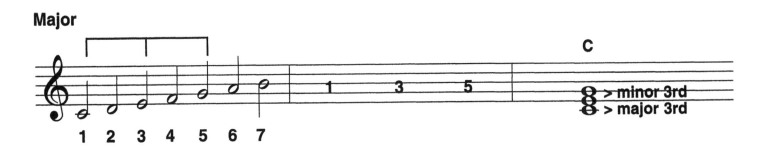

**Minor**

**Diminished**

**Augmented**

# MAJOR SCALE CHART

| Scale | 1 | 2 | 3 | 4 | 5 | 6 | 7 | 8 |
|-------|-----|-----|-----|-----|-----|-----|-----|-----|
| C | C | D | E | F | G | A | B | C |
| G | G | A | B | C | D | E | F# | G |
| D | D | E | F# | G | A | B | C# | D |
| A | A | B | C# | D | E | F# | G# | A |
| E | E | F# | G# | A | B | C# | D# | E |
| B | B | C# | D# | E | F# | G# | A# | B |
| F# | F# | G# | A# | B | C# | D# | E# | F# |
| F | F | G | A | Bb | C | D | E | F |
| Bb | Bb | C | D | Eb | F | G | A | Bb |
| Eb | Eb | F | G | Ab | Bb | C | D | Eb |
| Ab | Ab | Bb | C | Db | Eb | F | G | Ab |
| Db | Db | Eb | F | Gb | Ab | Bb | C | Db |
| Gb | Gb | Ab | Bb | Cb | Db | Eb | F | Gb |

The Major Scale Chart above lists the major scales. Every note in each scale is shown with its degree (or number). A sharp (#) symbol means to raise (R) a note by one half-step. A flat (b) symbol means to lower (L) a note by one half-step.

**To transpose chords** from one key to another:
- Find the chord in the original key
- Staying in the same column, go to the row of the new key
- Read the new chord name

**To make chords not pictured in this book** use the Major Scale Chart above and the Chord Building Chart on the opposite page.
- Identify the chord and find the formula from the Chord Building Chart.
- Find the name of the chord in the left column on the Major Scale Chart.
- Follow the formula moving through the scale and play the corresponding notes.

# CHORD BUILDING CHART

| CHORD | NOTES |
|---|---|
| Major | 1 - 3 - 5 |
| Major Flat Five (-5) | 1 - 3 - b5 |
| Major Add Nine (add 9) | 1 - 3 - 5 - 9 |
| Suspended (sus) | 1 - 4 - 5 |
| Fifth (5) | 1 - 5 |
| Minor (m) | 1 - b3 - 5 |
| Augmented (+) | 1 - 3 - #5 |
| Diminished (dim) | 1 - b3 - b5 |
| | |
| Sixth (6) | 1 - 3 - 5 - 6 |
| Sixth Add Nine (6/9) | 1 - 3 - 5 - 6 - 9 |
| Minor Sixth (m6) | 1 - b3 - 5 - 6 |
| Minor Sixth Add Nine (m6/9) | 1 - b3 - 5 - 6 - 9 |
| | |
| Seventh (Dominant) (7) | 1 - 3 - 5 - b7 |
| Seventh Suspended (7sus) | 1 - 4 - 5 - b7 |
| Seventh Augmented Five (7+5) | 1 - 3 - #5 - b7 |
| Seventh Diminished | 1 - b3 - b5 - bb7 |
| Seventh Diminished Five (7-5) | 1 - 3 - b5 - b7 |
| Seventh Augmented Nine (7+9) | 1 - 3 - 5 - b7 - #9 |
| Seventh Diminished Nine (7-9) | 1 - 3 - 5 - b7 - b9 |
| Seventh Augmented Five Flat Nine (7+5-9) | 1 - 3 - #5 - b7 - b9 |
| Major Seventh (maj7) | 1 - 3 - 5 - 7 |
| Minor Seventh (m7) | 1 - b3 - 5 - b7 |
| Minor Seventh Diminished Five (m7-5) | 1 - b3 - b5 - b7 |
| Minor Major Seventh (m,maj7) | 1 - b3 - 5 - 7 |
| | |
| Ninth (Dominant) (9) | 1 - 3 - 5 - b7 - 9 |
| Minor Ninth (m9) | 1 - b3 - 5 - b7 - 9 |
| Ninth Augmented Five (9+5) | 1 - 3 - #5 - b7 - 9 |
| Ninth Diminished Five (9-5) | 1 - 3 - b5 - b7 - 9 |
| Major Ninth (maj9) | 1 - 3 - 5 - 7 - 9 |
| Ninth Augmented Eleventh (9+11) | 1 - 3 - 5 - b7 - 9 - #11 |
| Minor Ninth Major Seventh (m9,maj7) | 1 - b3 - 5 - 7 - 9 |
| | |
| Eleventh (11) | 1 - 3 - 5 - b7 - 9 - 11 |
| Minor Eleventh (m11) | 1 - b3 - 5 - b7 - 9 - 11 |
| | |
| Thirteenth (13) | 1 - 3 - 5 - b7 - 9 - 11 - 13 |
| Thirteenth Diminished Nine (13-9) | 1 - 3 - 5 - b7 - b9 - 11 - 13 |
| Thirteenth Diminished Five Diminished Nine (13-5-9) | 1 - 3 - b5 - b7 - b9 - 11 - 13 |
| Minor Thirteenth (m13) | 1 - b3 - 5 - b7 - 9 - 11 - 13 |

Note:

    (+) and (#) are both used to mean raise a note by one half-step
    (-) and (b) are both used to mean lower a note by one half-step

# INFO PAGE

- Enharmonic equivalents sound the same but are written differently.

   For example: C# and Db

- When the bass note is other than the name of the chord, it is indicated after the chord symbol and a slash.

   For example: C/E means play C chord with an E bass (lowest note).

- Here is a chart to help you remember the topography (shape) of the major triads in the root position.

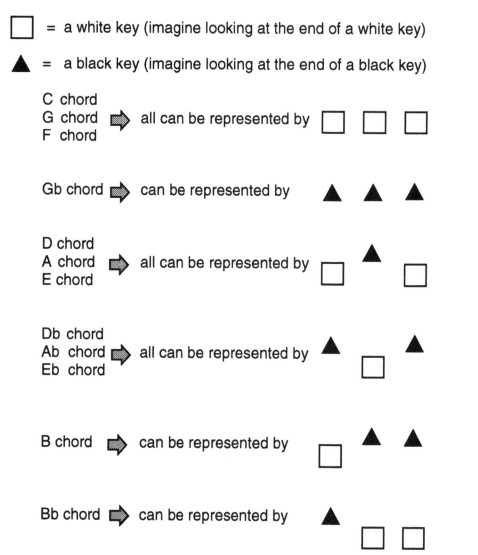

☐ = a white key (imagine looking at the end of a white key)

▲ = a black key (imagine looking at the end of a black key)

C chord
G chord ➡ all can be represented by ☐ ☐ ☐
F chord

Gb chord ➡ can be represented by ▲ ▲ ▲

D chord
A chord ➡ all can be represented by ☐ ▲ ☐
E chord

Db chord
Ab chord ➡ all can be represented by ▲ ☐ ▲
Eb chord

B chord ➡ can be represented by ☐ ▲ ▲

Bb chord ➡ can be represented by ▲ ☐ ☐

# MORE INFO

## Metronome Settings (Beats per Minute)

| | | |
|---|---|---|
| 40 -- 60 | Largo (broad) | |
| 60 -- 66 | Larghetto (a diminutive of Largo) | |
| 66 -- 76 | Adagio (slow; literally, at ease) | |
| 76 -- 108 | Andante (walking) | |
| 108 -- 120 | Moderato (moderate) | |
| 120 -- 168 | Allegro (fast; literally, cheerful) | |
| 168 -- 200 | Presto (very fast) | |
| 200 -- 208 | Prestissimo (as fast as possible) | |

In addition to these are terms calling for gradual change of speed, mainly *ritardando* (slackening), and *accelerando* (quickening).

*Rubato* - indicates a delicate unsteadiness of tempo.

## Other Names For Scale Degrees

For the key of C:

| | | | | |
|---|---|---|---|---|
| C | 1 | I | Tonic | Do |
| D | 2 | II | Supertonic | Re |
| E | 3 | III | Mediant | Mi |
| F | 4 | IV | Subdominant | Fa |
| G | 5 | V | Dominant | Sol |
| A | 6 | VI | Submediant | La |
| B | 7 | VII | Subtonic (leading tone) | Ti (Si) |
| C' | 8 | I | Tonic | Do |

- Arabic numbers (e.g., 1, 5) are used in music for fingering, counting, and degrees in a scale as building blocks for chords.

- Roman numerals (e.g., I, V) are used in music theory to indicate the chords in a scale. The first chord in any scale is I, the fifth chord V. The Roman numeral indicates not only the degree of the scale, but all the notes that go along with that chord.

- Sometimes, Arabic and Roman numerals are both used, as in the dominant seventh (V7) chord. The common name for the dominant seventh is the seventh chord (e.g., G7). The dominant seventh leads back to the I or tonic chord (e.g., G7 resolves to C).

# CIRCLE OF KEYS

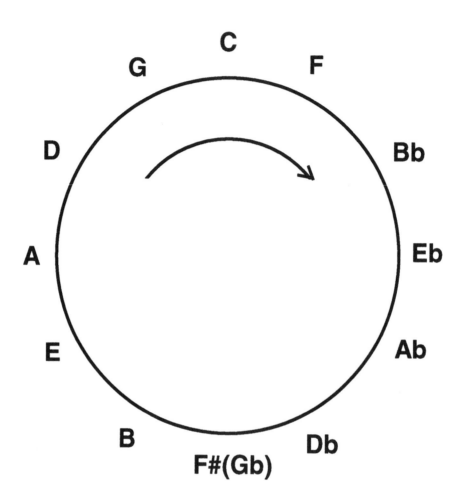

- If you make a 7th out of any chord, it will lead to the next chord on the right.

- Point to a key. This is the **I** chord. The chord on the left is the **V** chord. The chord on the right is the **IV** chord. The **I**, **IV**, and **V** chords are the most frequently used chords in songs.

- Here's a way to remember the Circle of Keys:
    **C** is for Christ, **F** is for Father. Rosary beads
    (**B**b,**E**b,**A**b,**D**b) take you to Father and God,
    Who are One (**F**#/**G**b). Rosary beads (**B,E,A,D**)
    lead you back to God (**G**).